THE ULTIMATE
TAX LIENS
AND DEEDS
INVESTING
GUIDE

Build Wealth Through Real Estate with
Low-Risk, High-Reward Investments
Strategies for Securing High Returns

Robert Newton

© Copyright 2024 - All rights reserved.

The content contained within this book may not be reproduced, duplicated, or transmitted without direct written permission from the author or the publisher.

Under no circumstances will any blame or legal responsibility be held against the publisher, or author, for any damages, reparation, or monetary loss due to the information contained within this book. Either directly or indirectly.

Legal Notice:

This book is copyright protected. This book is only for personal use. You cannot amend, distribute, sell, use, quote, or paraphrase any part, or the content within this book, without the consent of the author or publisher.

Disclaimer Notice:

By reading this document, the reader agrees that under no circumstances is the author responsible for any losses, direct or indirect, which are incurred as a result of the use of the information contained within this document, including, but not limited to, — errors, omissions, or inaccuracies.

TABLE OF CONTENTS

Preface 1

Introduction 4
    1. Why Tax Liens and Deeds Investing? 4
    2. Common Misconceptions 6
    3. The Potential for Passive Income 8

Chapter 1: Understanding Tax Liens and Deeds 11
    1. What Are Tax Liens and Tax Deeds? 11
    2. How Do They Work? 13
    3. Why Governments Use Them 15
    4. The Benefits for Investors 17
    5. Legal and Regulatory Considerations (the most up-to-date and recent information possible) 19

Chapter 2: Getting Started with Tax Liens 21
    1. The Investment Mindset 21
    2. Choosing Your Investment Strategy 23
    3. The Budget for Beginners 24
    4. Self-Directed IRAs and Tax Liens (the most up-to-date and recent information possible) 26
    5. Researching Your Target Areas 28

Chapter 3: Mastering Tax Deed Auctions 30
    1. What to Expect at an Auction 30
    2. How to Win at Auctions 32
    3. Researching Properties Before the Auction 33
    4. What Happens After You Win 35
    5. Flipping or Holding Properties 37

Chapter 4: Buying Tax Lien Certificates 39

1. How to Purchase a Tax Lien Certificate 39
2. Understanding Interest Rates and Redemption 41
3. What Happens When a Lien is Redeemed 42
4. The Foreclosure Process 44
5. Risks and Rewards 46

Chapter 5: The States that Sell Tax Liens 48

1. An Overview of Tax Lien States 48
2. How Each State Differs (the most up-to-date and recent information possible) 50
3. Best States for Beginners 51
4. How to Participate in Out-of-State Auctions 53
5. Building a Multi-State Portfolio 55

Chapter 6: Tax Deed Investing and Profits 57

1. What Happens After Acquiring a Deed 57
2. Renovation or Sale? 59
3. Flipping Tax Deed Properties 60
4. Holding for Long-Term Gains 62
5. Success Stories 64

Chapter 7: Avoiding Common Pitfalls 66

1. The Most Common Mistakes Investors Make 66
2. How to Conduct Thorough Due Diligence 68
3. Recognizing Red Flags 69
4. Working with Professionals 71
5. Learning from Failure 73

Chapter 8: Financing Your Investments 75

1. Using Investor Funds 75
2. Self-Funding Your Investment 77
3. Loans and Lines of Credit (the most up-to-date and recent information possible) 78
4. Leveraging Equity from Other Properties 80
5. The Power of Compound Growth 81

Chapter 9: Tax Implications and Planning 84

1. Understanding Tax Laws (the most up-to-date and recent information possible) 84
2. Tax Liens and Tax-Free Growth in IRAs 86
3. Handling Capital Gains 87
4. Tracking Your Investments for Tax Purposes 89
5. Working with a Tax Professional 90

Chapter 10: Long-Term Success Strategies 93

1. Scaling Your Investment Portfolio 93
2. Diversifying Investments 95
3. Investing in Multiple Markets 96
4. Building a Passive Income Stream 98
5. Managing Your Portfolio Like a Pro 100

Chapter 11: Advanced Techniques for Experienced Investors 102

1. How to Buy Properties Before They Go to Auction 102
2. Insider Secrets to Doubling Returns 104
3. Using Technology to Enhance Your Investments (the most up-to-date and recent information possible) 105
4. Building Relationships with Local Authorities 107
5. Staying Ahead of the Competition 109

Chapter 12: Real-Life Success Stories and Case Studies 111

1. Inspiring Success Stories 111
2. Overcoming Challenges 113
3. Turning Small Investments into Large Profits 114
4. Strategies That Worked 116
5. What You Can Learn from Their Journeys 118

Conclusion 120

PREFACE

Welcome to "The Ultimate Tax Liens and Deeds Investing Guide: Build Wealth Through Real Estate with Low-Risk, High-Reward Investments Strategies for Securing High Returns." I am Robert Newton, your guide on this journey towards financial freedom and wealth creation. As a seasoned real estate investor and author, my goal is to demystify the world of tax liens and deeds investing, offering you the knowledge and tools you need to succeed.

This book is designed to be a comprehensive guide, providing you with the necessary insights and strategies to navigate the profitable yet often misunderstood realm of tax liens and deeds. Whether you're an aspiring investor, an experienced portfolio manager, a retiree seeking passive income, a real estate enthusiast, or a side hustler looking for a lucrative investment avenue, this book is tailored to meet your needs.

The world of tax liens and deeds investing is filled with potential. These low-risk, high-reward investment opportunities can yield impressive returns, even for those starting with modest capital.

However, like any investment, they require a clear understanding of the laws, regulations, and strategies involved. This book is designed to provide you with that understanding, breaking down complex concepts into digestible, actionable steps.

In the chapters that follow, we will delve into the intricacies of tax liens and deeds, exploring how they work, their benefits for investors, and the legal considerations involved. We will guide you through the process of getting started, mastering tax deed auctions, buying tax lien certificates, and navigating the different tax lien and deed states. We will also equip you with strategies for long-term success, including how to avoid common pitfalls, finance your investments, handle tax implications, and scale your portfolio.

Throughout the book, we will maintain an authoritative yet accessible tone, ensuring that even beginners can grasp these complex concepts. We will also share real-life success stories and case studies, offering you practical examples and inspiration for your own investment journey.

It's important to note that while tax liens and deeds investing can be lucrative, it's not a get-rich-quick scheme. Success in this field requires patience, diligence, and a strategic approach. However, with the right knowledge and guidance, it is a viable path to building wealth and achieving financial freedom.

As we embark on this journey together, I encourage you to approach each chapter with an open mind and a willingness to learn. Remember, the road to financial success is not always straightforward, but with the right tools and knowledge, you can navigate it with confidence.

In the ever-evolving world of real estate investing, staying ahead of the curve is crucial. This book will not only provide you with up-to-date industry knowledge but also prepare you for the future, exploring how technology can enhance your investment approach in 2024/2025.

I am excited to share this journey with you and look forward to helping you unlock the potential of tax liens and deeds investing. Let's embark on this journey towards financial freedom and wealth creation together.

Robert Newton

INTRODUCTION

1. Why Tax Liens and Deeds Investing?

As we embark on this journey into the world of tax liens and deeds investing, it's crucial to understand why this particular investment avenue is worth exploring. The world of investing is vast and varied, offering a plethora of options for those seeking to grow their wealth. From stocks and bonds to real estate and mutual funds, the choices can often seem overwhelming. However, amidst this wide array of options, tax liens and deeds stand out for several compelling reasons.

Firstly, tax liens and deeds offer a unique blend of low risk and high potential returns. When you invest in a tax lien or deed, you're essentially paying someone else's overdue property taxes. In return, you receive the right to collect these taxes, plus interest, from the property owner. If the owner fails to repay within a specified period, you can foreclose on the property, often acquiring it for a fraction of its market value. This mechanism provides a safety net that few other investments can match. Even in the worst-case scenario, where the property owner fails to repay the taxes, you still stand to gain a valuable piece of real estate.

Moreover, tax liens and deeds are backed by the government, adding an extra layer of security to your investment. Unlike stocks or mutual funds, which can fluctuate wildly based on market conditions, tax liens and deeds offer a more stable and predictable return. This stability makes them an attractive option for investors seeking to mitigate risk while still achieving substantial returns.

Another compelling reason to consider tax liens and deeds investing is the relatively low entry barrier. Unlike other forms of real estate investing, which often require significant upfront capital, tax liens and deeds can be acquired with a relatively small investment. This accessibility opens the door for a wider range of investors, including those who may not have substantial savings to invest.

Tax liens and deeds also offer a degree of flexibility that is often lacking in other investment options. As an investor, you have the option to either hold onto the lien or deed, earning interest over time, or foreclose on the property and potentially sell it for a profit. This flexibility allows you to adapt your strategy based on your financial goals and market conditions.

Furthermore, tax liens and deeds investing is a field that is still relatively untapped. While other forms of investing are highly competitive, tax liens and deeds remain a niche market. This lack of competition can work in your favor, allowing you to acquire liens and deeds at lower prices and with less bidding competition.

Lastly, tax liens and deeds investing is a field that rewards research and due diligence. Unlike the stock market, where information is readily available and often priced into the stocks, tax liens and deeds require a more hands-on approach. This research can include everything from assessing the property's value to understanding local tax laws. While this may seem daunting, it also provides an opportunity. Those willing to put in the time and effort to thoroughly research their investments can often uncover lucrative opportunities that others may overlook.

Tax liens and deeds investing offers a unique opportunity for investors seeking a low-risk, high-reward investment option. With its combination of government backing, potential for high returns, low entry barrier, flexibility, lack of competition, and reward for due diligence, it's an investment avenue well worth considering. Whether you're a seasoned investor looking to diversify your portfolio or a beginner seeking a stable and profitable investment, tax liens and deeds investing could be the key to unlocking your financial potential.

2. Common Misconceptions

As we delve deeper into the world of tax liens and deeds investing, it's crucial to address some of the common misconceptions that often surround this investment strategy. Misunderstandings and misinformation can deter potential investors, leading them to miss out on the lucrative opportunities that tax liens and deeds investing can offer.

One of the most prevalent misconceptions is that tax liens and deeds investing is overly complicated and only suitable for experienced investors. While it's true that this form of investing involves certain complexities, it's far from inaccessible. Like any investment strategy, it requires a solid understanding of the underlying principles and processes. However, with the right knowledge and guidance, even novice investors can navigate the world of tax liens and deeds successfully. This book aims to provide that guidance, breaking down complex concepts into digestible, actionable insights.

Another common misconception is that tax liens and deeds investing is a high-risk strategy. This stems from a misunderstanding of the nature of these investments. When you invest in a tax lien or deed, you're not buying the property itself, but a claim on the property due to unpaid taxes. This claim is backed by the government, which significantly reduces the risk. If the property owner fails to pay their taxes, the investor can recoup their investment through the sale of the property. This safety net makes tax liens and deeds one of the lower-risk forms of real estate investing.

A third misconception is that tax liens and deeds investing requires a significant amount of capital. In reality, this form of investing is accessible to those with modest funds. While the exact amount needed will depend on the specific tax lien or deed, it's possible to start investing with a few thousand dollars. This makes tax liens and deeds investing a viable option for those looking to dip their toes into the world of real estate investing without a substantial initial outlay.

The belief that tax liens and deeds investing is a quick way to make money is another misconception that needs to be addressed. While it's true that these investments can offer high returns, they're not typically a fast track to wealth. The process from purchasing a tax lien or deed to receiving a return on your investment can take anywhere from a few months to a few years, depending on the redemption period set by the state. Patience and a long-term investment mindset are key to success in tax liens and deeds investing.

Finally, there's a misconception that tax liens and deeds investing is a surefire way to acquire real estate at rock-bottom prices. While it's true that these investments can lead to the acquisition of property, this is not the norm. Most property owners eventually pay their taxes, and the investor earns interest on their investment rather than acquiring the property. While acquiring property through tax liens and deeds can happen, it's important to approach these investments primarily as a source of interest income, not as a guaranteed path to acquiring real estate.

In debunking these misconceptions, my aim is not to paint an overly rosy picture of tax liens and deeds investing. Like any investment strategy, it has its risks and challenges. However, with a clear understanding of what these investments entail, you can make informed decisions and develop strategies that maximize returns while mitigating risks. As we continue our journey through this book, we'll delve deeper into these strategies, equipping you with the knowledge and tools you need to succeed in the world of tax liens and deeds investing.

3. The Potential for Passive Income

As we continue our exploration of tax liens and deeds investing, it's important to highlight one of the most appealing aspects of this investment avenue: the potential for passive income. In the world of investing, passive income is often seen as the holy grail. It's income that requires little to no effort to maintain, providing a steady stream of earnings that can supplement your regular income, fund your retirement, or even allow you to achieve financial independence.

So, how do tax liens and deeds contribute to passive income? Let's start with tax liens. When you invest in a tax lien, you're essentially lending money to the property owner to pay their unpaid taxes. In return, you receive the right to collect these taxes, plus interest, from the property owner. This interest is where the potential for passive income lies. Once you've purchased a tax lien, the interest accrues automatically, without any additional effort on your part. All you have to do is wait for the property owner to repay their taxes, at which point you receive your initial investment back, plus the accrued interest.

The interest rates on tax liens can be quite lucrative, often ranging from 8% to 36% per year, depending on the state. This can provide a steady stream of income, significantly higher than what you might earn from a savings account or other low-risk investments. And if the property owner fails to repay their taxes within the redemption period, you have the right to foreclose on the property, potentially acquiring it for a fraction of its market value. This property can then be rented out or sold, providing another source of passive income.

Tax deeds, on the other hand, offer a different path to passive income. When you buy a tax deed, you're buying ownership of the property itself. This property can then be rented out, providing a steady stream of rental income. Alternatively, you can sell the property, potentially for a significant profit if you managed to buy it for less than its market value.

However, it's important to note that while tax deeds can offer substantial returns, they also require more active management than tax liens. As the property owner, you're responsible for maintaining the property, finding tenants, and dealing with any issues that arise. Therefore, while tax deeds can provide passive income, they also require a more hands-on approach.

Whether you choose to invest in tax liens, tax deeds, or a combination of both, the potential for passive income is clear. With a strategic approach and careful research, you can build a portfolio of investments that provides a steady stream of income, requiring little to no ongoing effort to maintain.

However, it's important to remember that while tax liens and deeds offer the potential for passive income, they're not a get-rich-quick scheme. Success in this field requires patience, diligence, and a strategic approach. The returns may not be immediate, and there are risks involved, as with any investment. But for those willing to put in the time and effort to understand this market, the rewards can be substantial.

The potential for passive income is one of the most appealing aspects of tax liens and deeds investing. Whether through the interest on tax liens or the rental income from tax deed properties, these investments offer a path to financial freedom that few other investments can match. With the right knowledge and strategy, you can use tax liens and deeds to build a stream of passive income, supplementing your regular income, funding your retirement, or even allowing you to achieve financial independence.

Chapter 1

UNDERSTANDING TAX LIENS AND DEEDS

1. What Are Tax Liens and Tax Deeds?

As we delve into the first chapter of our journey into tax liens and deeds investing, it's crucial to establish a solid understanding of what these terms mean. While we've touched on these concepts in the introduction, let's take a more in-depth look.

Tax liens and tax deeds are both mechanisms used by local governments to recover unpaid property taxes. However, they operate differently and offer distinct opportunities for investors. Understanding these differences is key to crafting a successful investment strategy.

A tax lien is a legal claim made by the government against a property when the property owner fails to pay their property taxes. This lien ensures that the owed taxes must be paid before the property can be sold or refinanced. The government can then sell this lien to investors in the form of a tax lien certificate. This certificate represents the investor's right to collect the unpaid taxes, plus interest, from the property owner.

The interest rate on tax liens can be quite lucrative, often ranging from 8% to 36% per year, depending on the state. This interest accrues over time, providing a steady return on investment. If the property owner fails to repay their taxes within a specified redemption period, the holder of the tax lien certificate can foreclose on the property, potentially acquiring it for the amount of unpaid taxes.

On the other hand, a tax deed is a legal document that grants ownership of a property to the government when the property owner fails to pay their taxes. In states that use the tax deed system, the government doesn't sell tax lien certificates. Instead, it sells the property itself to recover the unpaid taxes. This sale, known as a tax deed sale, is usually conducted as an auction, with the property going to the highest bidder.

When you buy a tax deed, you're buying ownership of the property. This can offer substantial returns, as the starting bid is often just the amount of unpaid taxes, which can be significantly less than the property's market value. However, as the new owner, you're also responsible for any issues with the property, from structural problems to legal disputes. This makes due diligence crucial when investing in tax deeds.

In essence, tax liens and tax deeds represent two sides of the same coin. Both are tools used by governments to recover unpaid property taxes, and both offer opportunities for investors. However, they require different strategies and carry different levels of risk and reward.

Tax liens offer a more passive investment, with the potential for steady returns through interest payments and the possibility of acquiring a property if the owner fails to repay their taxes. Tax deeds, on the other hand, offer the opportunity to acquire properties at potentially steep discounts, but require more active management and carry more risk.

Understanding these differences is the first step in your journey into tax liens and deeds investing. With this knowledge, you can begin to evaluate which approach is right for you, based on your financial goals, risk tolerance, and investment style. Whether you choose to invest in tax liens, tax deeds, or a combination of both, these investments offer a unique opportunity to build wealth and achieve financial freedom.

2. How Do They Work?

Now that we have a fundamental understanding of what tax liens and tax deeds are, it's time to delve into the mechanics of how they work. This understanding is crucial, as it forms the foundation upon which successful investing strategies are built.

Let's start with tax liens. When a property owner fails to pay their property taxes, the government places a lien on the property. This lien is essentially a legal claim against the property, ensuring that the unpaid taxes will be paid before the property can be sold or refinanced. However, rather than waiting for the property owner to pay these taxes, the government opts to sell tax lien certificates to investors.

When you buy a tax lien certificate, you're essentially stepping into the shoes of the government. You pay the unpaid taxes and, in return, you receive the right to collect these taxes, plus interest, from the property owner. The interest rate is set by the state and can range from 8% to 36% per year. This interest accrues over time, providing a steady return on your investment.

If the property owner repays their taxes within the redemption period, which can range from a few months to a few years depending on the state, you receive your initial investment back, plus the accrued interest. If they fail to repay within this period, you can initiate foreclosure proceedings to acquire the property.

Now, let's turn to tax deeds. In states that use the tax deed system, the government doesn't sell tax lien certificates. Instead, it sells the property itself to recover the unpaid taxes. This sale, known as a tax deed sale, is usually conducted as an auction.

When you buy a tax deed, you're buying ownership of the property. The starting bid is typically the amount of unpaid taxes, which can be significantly less than the property's market value. This can offer substantial returns if you're able to sell the property at its market value. However, as the new owner, you're also responsible for any issues with the property, from structural problems to legal disputes.

It's important to note that tax deed sales are final. Once the sale is complete, the previous owner has no right to reclaim the property. However, some states offer a redemption period after the tax deed sale, during which the previous owner can repay the unpaid taxes and reclaim the property. This is known as a redeemable deed.

In both tax liens and tax deeds, the key to success lies in thorough research and due diligence. Understanding the property's value, the local real estate market, and the legal processes involved is crucial. This research can include everything from assessing the property's condition and location to reviewing title reports and local tax laws.

Tax liens and tax deeds operate on the same fundamental principle: the government's need to recover unpaid property taxes. However, they offer different opportunities for investors. Tax liens provide a more passive investment with the potential for steady returns, while tax deeds offer the opportunity to acquire properties at potentially steep discounts. Understanding how these mechanisms work is the first step towards crafting a successful investment strategy in this lucrative market.

3. Why Governments Use Them

As we continue our exploration of tax liens and tax deeds, it's essential to understand why governments use these mechanisms. At first glance, it might seem counterintuitive. Why would a government sell a lien or a deed for unpaid taxes instead of waiting for the property owner to pay? The answer lies in the financial realities that local governments face and the role that property taxes play in their budgets.

Property taxes are a vital source of revenue for local governments. They fund essential services like schools, roads, police and fire departments, parks, and other community resources. When property owners fail to pay their taxes, it creates a budget shortfall. This can lead to cuts in services, delays in infrastructure projects, and other negative impacts on the community.

However, collecting unpaid taxes can be a lengthy and costly process. It involves legal proceedings, administrative work, and potential court costs. Even after a lien has been placed on a property, there's no guarantee of when, or even if, the taxes will be paid. This uncertainty makes it difficult for governments to plan their budgets and ensure the provision of essential services.

This is where tax liens and tax deeds come into play. By selling tax lien certificates or tax deeds, governments can recover the unpaid taxes quickly and efficiently. This allows them to fill budget gaps, fund essential services, and maintain financial stability.

When a government sells a tax lien certificate, it receives the unpaid taxes immediately. The investor who buys the certificate then assumes the risk of collecting the taxes from the property owner. This arrangement benefits the government by providing immediate revenue and reducing administrative costs.

Tax deed sales work on a similar principle. When a government sells a tax deed, it recovers the unpaid taxes through the sale of the property. This not only provides immediate revenue but also transfers the responsibility of property ownership and maintenance to the investor.

In both cases, the government recovers the unpaid taxes without having to wait for the property owner to pay or go through the costly and time-consuming process of foreclosure. This makes tax liens and tax deeds an effective tool for governments to manage their finances and ensure the provision of essential services.

However, it's important to note that governments don't take the decision to sell tax liens or tax deeds lightly. Property taxes are a matter of public record, and property owners are given ample notice of their unpaid taxes and the consequences of non-payment. Governments typically resort to selling tax liens or tax deeds only after multiple attempts to collect the taxes have failed.

Governments use tax liens and tax deeds as a tool to manage their finances, recover unpaid taxes, and ensure the provision of essential services. For investors, these mechanisms offer unique opportunities to earn high returns and potentially acquire properties at a discount. Understanding why governments use tax liens and tax deeds can provide valuable insights into the market dynamics and potential opportunities in this field.

4. The Benefits for Investors

As we delve deeper into the mechanics of tax liens and tax deeds, it's essential to highlight the numerous benefits these investment avenues offer. While the intricacies of these investments may seem daunting initially, the potential rewards make them an attractive option for a wide range of investors.

One of the most appealing aspects of investing in tax liens is the potential for high returns. The interest rates on tax liens can be quite lucrative, often ranging from 8% to 36% per year, depending on the state. This interest accrues over time, providing a steady return on your investment. If the property owner repays their taxes within the redemption period, you receive your initial investment back, plus the accrued interest. This can provide a steady stream of income, significantly higher than what you might earn from a savings account or other low-risk investments.

Moreover, if the property owner fails to repay their taxes within the redemption period, you have the right to foreclose on the property. This can lead to potentially acquiring a property for a fraction of its market value, offering a significant return on your investment.

Investing in tax deeds also presents its own set of advantages. When you buy a tax deed, you're buying ownership of the property. The starting bid is typically the amount of unpaid taxes, which can be significantly less than the property's market value. This can offer substantial returns if you're able to sell the property at its market value. Additionally, as the new owner, you have the option to rent the property, providing a steady stream of rental income.

Furthermore, tax liens and deeds offer diversification for your investment portfolio. They are a form of real estate investment, but they're different from traditional real estate investing. They offer a way to invest in real estate without the need for property management, renovations, or dealing with tenants, which are common aspects of traditional real estate investing. This makes tax liens and deeds an excellent way to diversify your portfolio and spread risk.

Another benefit of investing in tax liens and deeds is that they are relatively low-risk compared to other types of investments. The government regulates tax lien and deed sales, and the laws governing these sales are designed to protect investors. Additionally, because tax liens and deeds are tied to real estate, they are backed by a tangible asset. This means that even if the property owner fails to repay their taxes, you have a claim on a real asset that has intrinsic value.

Lastly, tax liens and deeds offer the opportunity for anyone to invest. While some forms of investing require significant capital, you can start investing in tax liens and deeds with a relatively small amount of money. This makes them an accessible investment option for a wide range of individuals.

The benefits of investing in tax liens and deeds are numerous. They offer the potential for high returns, portfolio diversification, low risk, and accessibility. However, like any investment, they require careful research and strategic planning. With a solid understanding of how tax liens and deeds work, and the benefits they offer, you can make informed decisions and build a successful investment strategy.

5. Legal and Regulatory Considerations (the most up-to-date and recent information possible)

As we further explore tax liens and tax deeds, it's crucial to understand the legal and regulatory considerations that come into play. These investments are governed by a complex web of laws and regulations that vary from state to state. Understanding these legalities is essential to navigate the investment landscape successfully and mitigate potential risks.

One of the most critical legal considerations when investing in tax liens or tax deeds is understanding the rights of the property owner. In most states, property owners have a redemption period during which they can repay their unpaid taxes, plus interest, to reclaim their property. This period varies by state, and understanding these timelines is crucial to your investment strategy.

Another key legal aspect is the priority of tax liens. In most jurisdictions, tax liens take precedence over other types of liens, such as mortgage liens. This means that if a property is sold to satisfy a tax lien, other lien holders may lose their claim on the property. This priority status makes tax liens a relatively secure investment.

When investing in tax deeds, it's important to understand that these sales are typically "as is." This means that you're responsible for any issues with the property, from structural problems to legal disputes. Due diligence, including a thorough title search, is essential to identify potential problems before bidding on a property.

In terms of regulatory considerations, tax lien and tax deed sales are usually conducted by local county governments and are subject to local laws and regulations. These can include requirements for public notice of the sale, bidding procedures, and payment methods. Some jurisdictions also have regulations regarding who can bid at these sales. For example, some states prohibit county employees or their relatives from bidding.

It's also worth noting that recent years have seen increased regulatory scrutiny of tax lien and tax deed sales. Some jurisdictions have implemented reforms aimed at protecting property owners, such as increased notice requirements or caps on interest rates. Staying up-to-date with these regulatory changes is crucial to ensure your investment strategy remains compliant and effective.

Investing in tax liens and tax deeds involves navigating a complex landscape of laws and regulations. Understanding these legal and regulatory considerations is key to mitigating risks and maximizing returns. It's always recommended to consult with a legal professional or a knowledgeable tax lien and deed advisor to ensure you're fully aware of the legal implications of your investments.

Chapter 2

GETTING STARTED WITH TAX LIENS

1. The Investment Mindset

As we embark on Chapter 2 of our journey into tax liens investing, it's crucial to begin with the right mindset. Investing in tax liens isn't a get-rich-quick scheme or a gamble. It's a strategic financial decision that requires patience, diligence, and a clear understanding of your financial goals and risk tolerance.

First and foremost, successful investing requires a long-term perspective. While tax liens can offer substantial returns, these returns may not be immediate. It can take months or even years for a property owner to repay their taxes and for you to receive your investment back, plus interest. In some cases, you may need to initiate foreclosure proceedings to recover your investment, which can be a lengthy and complex process. Patience and persistence are key.

Secondly, investing in tax liens requires a proactive approach to learning and research. The world of tax liens is complex and ever-changing, with laws and regulations varying from state to state and evolving over time. Successful investors are those who commit to ongoing education, staying up-to-date with the latest industry trends, legal changes, and market dynamics.

Risk management is another crucial aspect of the investment mindset. While tax liens are generally considered a low-risk investment, they're not risk-free. There's always the possibility that the property owner won't repay their taxes, or that the property's value won't cover your investment. Understanding these risks and taking steps to mitigate them, such as thorough due diligence and portfolio diversification, is essential.

Another key part of the investment mindset is understanding your financial goals and how tax liens fit into your overall investment strategy. Are you looking for a steady stream of income? Are you interested in potentially acquiring properties? How much risk are you willing to take on? Answering these questions can help you define your investment strategy and guide your decisions.

Lastly, successful investing requires discipline. This includes the discipline to stick to your investment strategy, even when faced with tempting opportunities that don't align with your goals or risk tolerance. It also includes the discipline to maintain a strict budget, avoiding the common pitfall of over-investing.

The right mindset is the foundation of successful investing in tax liens. This mindset involves a long-term perspective, a commitment to learning, a focus on risk management, a clear understanding of your financial goals, and the discipline to stick to your strategy and budget. With this mindset, you can navigate the world of tax liens investing with confidence and poise, maximizing your chances of achieving substantial returns.

2. Choosing Your Investment Strategy

With the right mindset in place, the next step in your tax lien investment journey is to choose your investment strategy. This strategy will serve as your roadmap, guiding your decisions and helping you navigate the complex landscape of tax lien investing.

There are several strategies you can adopt when investing in tax liens, each with its own risk and reward profile. The right strategy for you will depend on your financial goals, risk tolerance, and investment style.

One common strategy is the interest income strategy. This involves buying tax lien certificates with the aim of earning interest income. You're essentially acting as a lender, providing the government with the funds to cover unpaid taxes and earning interest in return. This strategy can provide a steady stream of income and is relatively low-risk, as your investment is secured by the property.

Another strategy is the property acquisition strategy. This involves buying tax lien certificates with the aim of acquiring the property if the owner fails to repay their taxes. This strategy can offer substantial returns, as you could potentially acquire a property for a fraction of its market value. However, it's also higher-risk and requires a more active approach, as you may need to initiate foreclosure proceedings and manage the property.

A third strategy is the hybrid strategy, which involves a mix of the interest income and property acquisition strategies. This can offer a balance of steady income and the potential for high returns, while spreading risk across multiple investments.

When choosing your investment strategy, it's important to consider your financial goals. Are you looking for a steady stream of income, or are you aiming for high returns? How much risk are you willing to take on? How active do you want to be in managing your investments? Your answers to these questions can help guide your choice of strategy.

It's also crucial to consider the legal and regulatory environment. The laws and regulations governing tax lien sales vary from state to state, and these can impact your strategy. For example, some states have high maximum interest rates, which can make the interest income strategy more lucrative. Others have short redemption periods, which can increase the chances of property acquisition.

Choosing your investment strategy is a key step in your tax lien investment journey. Whether you opt for the interest income strategy, the property acquisition strategy, or a hybrid approach, your strategy should align with your financial goals, risk tolerance, and investment style. With a clear strategy in place, you can make informed decisions, seize opportunities, and navigate the world of tax lien investing with confidence.

3. The Budget for Beginners

As we continue our journey into the world of tax lien investing, it's crucial to discuss the importance of budgeting. Whether you're a seasoned investor or a beginner, having a clear budget is a fundamental part of your investment strategy. It not only guides your investment decisions but also helps mitigate financial risks.

One of the appealing aspects of tax lien investing is its accessibility. Unlike other forms of real estate investing, tax lien investing doesn't require large amounts of capital. You can start investing in tax liens with a relatively small amount of money. However, it's important not to confuse accessibility with affordability. Just because you can start investing with a small amount doesn't mean you should invest all your available funds.

When setting your budget, the first step is to assess your financial situation. This involves taking a close look at your income, expenses, savings, and financial goals. How much money can you comfortably set aside for investing? Remember, investing always involves a degree of risk. You should never invest money that you can't afford to lose.

Next, consider the costs associated with tax lien investing. While the initial investment might be the purchase price of the tax lien, there are other costs to consider. These can include due diligence costs, such as the cost of title searches or property assessments, and potential legal fees if you need to foreclose on a property. You might also need to pay for property maintenance or improvements if you acquire a property.

Another key aspect of budgeting for tax lien investing is understanding the potential return on investment. This involves researching the interest rates and redemption periods in your target investment area. Remember, the return on investment isn't just the interest rate; it's also the time it takes to get your investment back. A high interest rate might seem attractive, but if the redemption period is long, your money could be tied up for years.

Lastly, it's important to regularly review and update your budget. Your financial situation and goals might change over time, and the tax lien market can also change. Regular reviews can help you stay on track and make necessary adjustments.

Budgeting is a crucial part of getting started with tax lien investing. It involves assessing your financial situation, understanding the costs and potential returns of tax lien investing, and regularly reviewing and updating your budget. With a clear budget, you can make informed investment decisions, manage financial risks, and set yourself up for success in the world of tax lien investing.

4. Self-Directed IRAs and Tax Liens (the most up-to-date and recent information possible)

As we delve deeper into the world of tax lien investing, it's important to discuss one of the lesser-known but highly advantageous methods of investing in tax liens: through a Self-Directed Individual Retirement Account (SDIRA). This unique investment vehicle offers a tax-advantaged way to invest in tax liens and can be a powerful tool for building wealth over the long term.

A Self-Directed IRA is a type of retirement account that offers the same tax benefits as a traditional or Roth IRA, but with one key difference: it allows you to invest in a broader range of assets, including real estate, private businesses, and, importantly for our discussion, tax liens.

Investing in tax liens through a SDIRA offers several benefits. First and foremost are the tax advantages. With a traditional SDIRA, your investments grow tax-deferred, meaning you don't pay taxes on your earnings until you start taking distributions in retirement. If you opt for a Roth SDIRA, your investments grow tax-free, meaning you won't pay taxes on your earnings at all, provided you meet certain conditions.

These tax advantages can significantly enhance the returns on your tax lien investments. The interest you earn from tax liens can compound over time, potentially leading to substantial growth in your retirement savings.

Another benefit of investing in tax liens through a SDIRA is the potential for diversification. By adding tax liens to your retirement portfolio, you can diversify your investments beyond the traditional stocks, bonds, and mutual funds. This can help spread risk and potentially enhance returns.

However, investing in tax liens through a SDIRA also comes with certain rules and considerations. For one, all investments and transactions must be made through the SDIRA, not personally. This means that the SDIRA must directly purchase the tax lien, and all income and expenses related to the tax lien must flow through the SDIRA.

Additionally, it's important to understand that tax lien investing through a SDIRA is a long-term strategy. The funds in your SDIRA are meant for retirement, and early withdrawals can result in taxes and penalties.

Finally, it's crucial to work with a knowledgeable SDIRA custodian. Not all custodians are familiar with tax lien investing, and it's essential to work with one who understands the process and can provide the necessary support and guidance.

Investing in tax liens through a Self-Directed IRA can offer a tax-advantaged way to enhance your retirement savings and diversify your investment portfolio. However, it's a strategy that requires careful planning and compliance with specific rules. As always, it's recommended to seek advice from a financial advisor or tax professional to ensure this strategy aligns with your overall financial goals and retirement plans.

5. Researching Your Target Areas

As we continue to explore the world of tax lien investing, the importance of researching your target areas cannot be overstated. The location of the properties associated with the tax liens you invest in can significantly impact your returns and overall investment experience.

One of the first things to consider when researching your target areas is the state's laws and regulations regarding tax liens. As we've discussed, these can vary widely from state to state. Some states offer high interest rates, while others have shorter redemption periods. Some states sell tax deeds instead of tax liens. Understanding these laws and regulations can help you identify the most lucrative and suitable investment opportunities.

Another important aspect to research is the local real estate market. The value of the properties associated with the tax liens can impact your potential returns, especially if you're considering the property acquisition strategy. Look at factors like property values, rental rates, and real estate market trends in your target areas.

You should also consider the economic conditions of your target areas. Areas with strong economies and job markets can be more likely to have property owners who can repay their taxes, which is important if you're aiming for the interest income strategy. On the other hand, areas with weaker economies may have more tax liens available, potentially offering more investment opportunities.

Finally, it's crucial to research the specific properties associated with the tax liens you're considering. This can involve checking the property's condition, looking up the property's title to check for other liens, and even visiting the property in person, if possible.

Researching your target areas is a crucial step in tax lien investing. It involves understanding the state's laws and regulations, assessing the local real estate and economic conditions, and researching the specific properties. With thorough research, you can make informed investment decisions and increase your chances of success in the world of tax lien investing.

Chapter 3

MASTERING TAX DEED AUCTIONS

1. What to Expect at an Auction

As we transition into the realm of tax deed auctions, it's important to set the stage for what to expect. Tax deed auctions can be exciting and potentially lucrative, but they can also be overwhelming for the uninitiated. Understanding the auction process and what to expect can help you navigate these auctions with confidence and poise.

Tax deed auctions are public auctions where tax-defaulted properties are sold to the highest bidder. They are typically conducted by the county government, either in a physical location such as a courthouse or online. The starting bid is usually the amount of unpaid taxes, interest, and penalties, which can be significantly less than the property's market value.

One of the first things to expect at a tax deed auction is competition. These auctions can attract a diverse crowd, from individual investors to seasoned real estate professionals. Everyone is there with the same goal: to acquire properties at a discount. This competition can drive up bid prices, so it's important to have a clear budget and stick to it.

Another thing to expect is a fast-paced environment. Auctions move quickly, and properties can be sold in a matter of minutes. It's crucial to stay focused and attentive, as missing a bid can mean missing out on a potential investment opportunity.

It's also important to know that all sales at tax deed auctions are final. Once the auctioneer's gavel falls, you're committed to the purchase. There's no opportunity to renegotiate the price or back out of the sale. This makes pre-auction research and due diligence absolutely crucial.

Payment terms at tax deed auctions can also be strict. Most auctions require payment in full immediately or within a short timeframe after the auction. Some auctions also require a deposit upfront. Be sure to understand the payment terms before you bid.

Finally, expect that there will be properties that don't sell at the auction. These properties, often called "over the counter" properties, may be available for purchase directly from the county after the auction. While these properties may have issues that made them less attractive to bidders, they can also present additional investment opportunities.

Tax deed auctions are a unique environment with their own set of rules and expectations. By understanding what to expect, you can navigate these auctions with confidence, making informed decisions and seizing opportunities. Remember, preparation is key. The more you know going into the auction, the better positioned you'll be to succeed.

2. How to Win at Auctions

Winning at tax deed auctions is both an art and a science. It involves careful preparation, strategic bidding, and a keen understanding of the auction dynamics. Here are some key strategies and tips to increase your chances of success.

Preparation is the cornerstone of winning at auctions. This involves researching the properties up for auction, understanding the auction rules and procedures, and setting a clear budget. When researching properties, look at factors like the property's condition, location, market value, and potential for profit. Understanding the auction rules can help you avoid costly mistakes, while setting a budget can prevent overbidding.

Strategic bidding is another crucial aspect of winning at auctions. One common strategy is to start with a low bid to test the competition. If there are no counterbids, you might be able to secure the property at a bargain price. If other bidders are present, you can gradually increase your bid, while always staying within your budget.

Timing is also important in bidding. Some experienced auction-goers recommend waiting until the last moment to place your bid, a strategy known as "sniping". This can catch other bidders off guard and reduce the chance of a bidding war. However, this strategy requires a keen sense of timing and a cool head.

Another key to winning at auctions is understanding the psychology of other bidders. If you can anticipate their strategies and reactions, you can adjust your bidding accordingly. For example, if you notice a bidder who seems to be emotionally attached to a property and determined to win at any cost, it might be wise to bow out and avoid a bidding war.

It's also important to stay flexible and adaptable. No two auctions are the same, and the dynamics can change quickly. A property that seemed unattractive at first might turn out to be a great investment opportunity, while a property that seemed like a sure bet might become overpriced due to fierce competition. Being able to adapt your strategy on the fly can give you an edge over less flexible bidders.

Finally, remember that winning isn't just about getting the highest bid. It's about securing a profitable investment. Winning a property at a high price might feel like a victory in the moment, but it can turn into a financial loss if the property turns out to be less valuable than you thought. Always keep your investment goals and budget in mind, and don't let the heat of the auction push you to make unwise decisions.

Winning at tax deed auctions involves a mix of careful preparation, strategic bidding, psychological insight, and flexibility. It's not an easy game, but with the right strategies and a cool head, you can increase your chances of success and secure profitable investments. Remember, every auction is a learning experience. The more auctions you attend, the more skilled you'll become, and the higher your chances of winning.

3. Researching Properties Before the Auction

As we delve deeper into the intricacies of tax deed auctions, it's crucial to emphasize the importance of researching properties before the auction. This research, often referred to as due diligence, is a critical step in the auction process. It can help you identify profitable investment opportunities, avoid potential pitfalls, and make informed bidding decisions.

The first step in researching properties is to obtain the list of properties up for auction. This list is usually available from the county government, either online or at the county office. The list typically includes information like the property's address, the amount of unpaid taxes, and the starting bid price.

Once you have the list, you can start researching individual properties. One of the first things to look at is the property's location. The location can significantly impact the property's value and its potential for profit. Consider factors like the neighborhood's desirability, local amenities, crime rates, and local real estate market conditions.

Next, try to assess the property's condition. This can be challenging, as you usually can't inspect the property in person before the auction. However, you can often get a sense of the property's condition from online property records, Google Street View, and local real estate listings. Look for signs of major issues, like structural damage or neglect.

Another crucial part of property research is checking the property's title. This involves looking for other liens or encumbrances on the property, such as mortgages, second liens, or easements. These can affect the property's value and your ability to sell or develop the property. Title research can be complex, so you might want to consider hiring a title company or real estate attorney to help.

You should also consider the property's potential for profit. This involves estimating the property's market value and potential rental income, and comparing these to the cost of the tax deed and any necessary repairs or improvements. Remember, the goal isn't just to acquire a property; it's to make a profitable investment.

Finally, it's important to understand that due diligence can't eliminate all risks. There's always a degree of uncertainty in tax deed investing, as you're often dealing with distressed properties and incomplete information. However, thorough research can significantly reduce these risks and increase your chances of success.

Researching properties before the auction is a critical step in tax deed investing. It involves assessing the property's location, condition, title, and potential for profit. While this research can be time-consuming and complex, it's a crucial part of making informed bidding decisions and securing profitable investments. Remember, the more you know about a property before the auction, the better equipped you'll be to bid wisely and win.

4. What Happens After You Win

The fall of the auctioneer's gavel and the declaration of your winning bid can be a thrilling moment. But winning the bid is just the beginning of your journey as a tax deed investor. Understanding what happens after you win is crucial to successfully navigating the post-auction process and ultimately profiting from your investment.

First and foremost, you'll need to pay for your winning bid. The payment terms can vary depending on the auction rules, but typically, you'll need to pay in full either immediately after the auction or within a short timeframe. Some auctions accept checks or wire transfers, while others might require certified funds. Late payment can result in penalties, or even forfeiture of the property, so it's crucial to have your finances in order and to understand the payment terms.

After payment, you'll receive a tax deed to the property. This deed transfers ownership of the property from the county to you. It's important to record this deed with the county recorder's office to officially establish your ownership.

However, receiving the tax deed doesn't necessarily mean you can start using or developing the property right away. Some states have a redemption period, during which the former owner can repay the unpaid taxes and reclaim the property. The length of this redemption period can vary, but it's typically between six months and two years. You'll need to wait until this redemption period expires before you can take full possession of the property.

Once the redemption period expires, you'll want to clear the property's title. Despite your ownership via the tax deed, other liens or claims on the property might still exist. Clearing the title can involve paying off these other liens or going through a legal process known as a quiet title action. This process can be complex, so you might want to consider hiring a real estate attorney to assist you.

Finally, once you have clear title to the property, you can decide what to do with it. If the property is in good condition, you might choose to rent it out for ongoing income. If it's in a desirable location, you might choose to sell it for a profit. If it needs work, you might choose to renovate it before selling or renting. Your strategy will depend on your investment goals, the property's condition and location, and the local real estate market.

Winning a bid at a tax deed auction is just the first step in your investment journey. What happens after you win involves paying for your bid, receiving and recording the tax deed, waiting out the redemption period, clearing the title, and deciding on your investment strategy. Each of these steps is crucial to successfully investing in tax deeds and ultimately achieving your investment goals. Remember, tax deed investing isn't just about winning at auctions; it's about what you do after you win that truly counts.

5. Flipping or Holding Properties

As we continue to unravel the intricacies of tax deed auctions, it's important to consider your strategy for the properties you acquire. Two common strategies are flipping properties and holding properties, each with its own potential benefits and considerations.

Flipping properties involves buying properties at a low price, often fixing them up, and then selling them for a profit. This strategy can be lucrative, especially if you're able to acquire properties significantly below market value at tax deed auctions and if you have the skills or resources to renovate properties affordably.

However, flipping properties also involves risks. Renovations can often be more costly and time-consuming than anticipated. The real estate market can fluctuate, and there's no guarantee that you'll be able to sell the property at a profit. It's also a more active form of investing, requiring time, effort, and management.

On the other hand, holding properties involves buying properties and then renting them out for ongoing income. This strategy can provide a steady stream of passive income, and you can also benefit from potential property appreciation over time.

Holding properties can be a good strategy if you're looking for long-term investment and if the properties are in areas with strong rental markets. It can also be a way to diversify your investment portfolio and hedge against inflation.

However, holding properties also comes with responsibilities and potential challenges. As a landlord, you'll be responsible for property maintenance, tenant management, and legal compliance. You'll also need to deal with vacancies, non-paying tenants, and potential property depreciation.

Whether you choose to flip or hold properties will depend on several factors. These can include your investment goals, risk tolerance, skills, resources, and the specifics of the property and local real estate market.

It's also worth noting that these strategies aren't mutually exclusive. You might choose to flip some properties and hold others, depending on the circumstances. Some investors even use a hybrid strategy, fixing up properties, renting them out for a while to generate income, and then selling them when the market conditions are favorable.

Deciding whether to flip or hold properties is a key consideration after winning at a tax deed auction. Each strategy has potential benefits and considerations, and the best choice depends on your individual circumstances and goals. Remember, successful real estate investing isn't just about acquiring properties; it's also about what you do with them after you acquire them.

Chapter 4

BUYING TAX LIEN CERTIFICATES

1. How to Purchase a Tax Lien Certificate

As we shift our focus to tax lien certificates, it's important to understand how to purchase them. Buying a tax lien certificate is a process that involves several steps, each with its own considerations and requirements.

The first step in purchasing a tax lien certificate is to identify the tax liens you're interested in. This involves researching the available tax liens, which are usually listed by the county government. These lists can often be found on the county's website or obtained directly from the county office. The list typically includes information like the property's address, the amount of unpaid taxes, and the interest rate.

Once you've identified the tax liens you're interested in, the next step is to participate in the tax lien sale. These sales are usually conducted as auctions, either in person or online. The bidding starts at the amount of the unpaid taxes, and the tax lien is sold to the highest bidder. It's important to understand the auction rules and procedures, as these can vary by county.

When bidding at the auction, it's crucial to have a clear budget and stick to it. The goal isn't just to win the auction, but to acquire a tax lien at a price that makes sense for your investment goals. Remember, the higher your bid, the lower your effective interest rate will be.

If you win the auction, you'll need to pay for your winning bid. The payment terms can vary depending on the auction rules, but typically, you'll need to pay in full either immediately after the auction or within a short timeframe. Some auctions accept checks or wire transfers, while others might require certified funds.

After payment, you'll receive the tax lien certificate. This certificate doesn't give you ownership of the property, but it does give you the right to collect the unpaid taxes, plus interest, from the property owner. If the owner doesn't pay within the redemption period, you can foreclose on the property.

Finally, it's important to understand that buying a tax lien certificate is an investment, and like all investments, it involves risk. The property owner might not pay the unpaid taxes, the property might be worth less than you thought, or there might be other liens or issues with the property. Thorough research and due diligence can help mitigate these risks, but they can't eliminate them entirely.

Purchasing a tax lien certificate involves identifying the tax liens you're interested in, participating in the tax lien sale, paying for your winning bid, and receiving the tax lien certificate. Each step requires careful planning, research, and decision-making. With the right approach, buying tax lien certificates can be a profitable investment strategy, offering the potential for high returns and the opportunity to acquire real estate at a discount.

2. Understanding Interest Rates and Redemption

As we delve deeper into the world of tax lien certificates, understanding interest rates and the redemption process is paramount. These elements play a significant role in the potential returns and overall dynamics of tax lien investing.

Interest rates on tax lien certificates can vary widely, depending on the state's laws and the specifics of the auction. Some states set a maximum interest rate, which can be as high as 18% or even 36% per year. Others use a bidding system where the interest rate is bid down, with the tax lien going to the bidder willing to accept the lowest interest rate. In some cases, the interest rate can be bid down to zero, with the bidder instead getting the right to foreclose on the property if the lien isn't redeemed.

The interest rate is important because it determines the return on your investment if the lien is redeemed. If you buy a tax lien certificate for $1,000 at an interest rate of 18%, and the lien is redeemed after six months, you'd earn $90 in interest. If the lien isn't redeemed, you have the right to foreclose on the property, potentially acquiring the property for far less than its market value.

The redemption process is another crucial aspect of tax lien investing. The redemption period is the time during which the property owner can pay the unpaid taxes, plus interest, to redeem the lien and prevent foreclosure. The length of the redemption period varies by state, but it's typically between six months and three years.

During the redemption period, you as the lien holder cannot do anything with the property. You can't sell it, improve it, or even set foot on it without the owner's permission. However, you do have the right to pay any subsequent taxes that become due, adding these amounts to your lien and earning interest on them.

If the redemption period expires without the lien being redeemed, you have the right to initiate foreclosure proceedings. This is a legal process that can be complex and costly, but it can also result in you acquiring the property. Once you own the property, you can sell it, rent it out, or use it as you wish.

However, it's important to understand that most tax liens are redeemed. Property owners have a strong incentive to redeem their liens, as failing to do so can result in losing their property. As a tax lien investor, your returns will most likely come from the interest you earn, not from acquiring properties through foreclosure.

Understanding interest rates and the redemption process is crucial to tax lien investing. The interest rate determines your potential returns, while the redemption process shapes the timeline and dynamics of your investment. By understanding these elements, you can make informed decisions and increase your chances of success in the world of tax lien certificates.

3. What Happens When a Lien is Redeemed

As we continue our journey into the world of tax lien certificates, it's crucial to understand what happens when a lien is redeemed.

This is a key event in the life cycle of a tax lien investment, and it has significant implications for your returns.

When a lien is redeemed, it means that the property owner, or possibly a mortgage lender or other interested party, has paid the unpaid taxes, plus interest and any penalties. This payment is made to the county, which then passes the funds on to you as the lien holder.

Redemption is good news for you as an investor. It means that your investment has paid off. You get your initial investment back, plus the interest. The rate of interest can be quite high, depending on the state's laws and the specifics of the auction. This interest is your profit on the investment.

When a lien is redeemed, the tax lien certificate is extinguished. You no longer have any claim on the property. The property owner gets a clear title back, free of your lien. This is the end of the investment cycle for that particular tax lien certificate.

The timing of the redemption can vary. It can happen at any time during the redemption period, which is set by state law and typically ranges from six months to three years. Most liens are redeemed well before the end of the redemption period. In fact, many are redeemed within the first few months, as property owners scramble to clear their title and avoid the threat of foreclosure.

The redemption process is typically handled by the county. You don't need to do anything to facilitate the redemption. However, you should keep track of your tax lien certificates and be aware of when the redemption period is nearing its end. If a lien isn't redeemed by the end of the redemption period, you have the right to initiate foreclosure proceedings.

When a lien is redeemed, it means that your investment has paid off. You get your initial investment back, plus interest, and the tax lien certificate is extinguished. While redemption ends your claim on the property, it also signifies a successful outcome for your investment. Understanding the redemption process and its implications can help you manage your tax lien portfolio effectively and maximize your returns.

4. The Foreclosure Process

While the majority of tax liens are redeemed before the end of the redemption period, there are instances where property owners fail to pay off their debt. In such cases, as a tax lien certificate holder, you have the right to initiate the foreclosure process. This process is complex and varies by state, but understanding its general outline is crucial for any tax lien investor.

Foreclosure is a legal process that allows you to take ownership of the property tied to your tax lien certificate. This process is initiated when the redemption period ends without the lien being redeemed. The aim of foreclosure is to recover the money you've invested, plus accrued interest, by selling the property.

The first step in the foreclosure process is usually to notify the property owner and any other interested parties. This typically involves sending a notice of intent to foreclose, which informs the property owner of your intent to take ownership of the property unless the lien is redeemed. The notice must be sent in a manner prescribed by state law, which often requires certified mail or personal delivery.

If the property owner still doesn't redeem the lien, the next step is usually to file a lawsuit in the county where the property is located.

This lawsuit, often called a foreclosure suit or a suit to quiet title, asks the court to grant you ownership of the property. You'll likely need a lawyer to help you navigate this process, as it involves complex legal procedures and paperwork.

During the lawsuit, the property owner and any other interested parties have the opportunity to contest the foreclosure. They might argue that the tax lien sale was invalid, that the lien has been paid, or that there are other reasons why the foreclosure should not proceed. If the court finds in their favor, the foreclosure process will be halted.

If the court finds in your favor, it will issue a judgment of foreclosure. This judgment gives you the right to take ownership of the property. However, before you can take ownership, there's usually a redemption period during which the property owner can still redeem the lien by paying the unpaid taxes, plus interest and costs. This redemption period varies by state, but it's typically between 30 days and six months.

If the lien isn't redeemed during this final redemption period, you can take ownership of the property. This typically involves recording the judgment of foreclosure with the county recorder's office. Once this is done, you're the legal owner of the property.

The foreclosure process is a complex legal process that allows you to take ownership of a property if a tax lien isn't redeemed. It involves notifying the property owner, filing a lawsuit, potentially going through a court battle, and finally taking ownership of the property. While this process can be time-consuming and costly, it can also result in you acquiring a property for significantly less than its market value. However, it's important to remember that most tax liens are redeemed, and foreclosure is the exception, not the rule.

5. Risks and Rewards

As we delve deeper into the intricacies of tax lien certificates, it is essential to understand the associated risks and rewards. Like any investment, tax lien certificates come with potential gains and pitfalls that must be carefully considered.

Let's start with the rewards. One of the primary attractions of tax lien certificates is the potential for high returns. The interest rates associated with tax liens can be significantly higher than those of traditional investments. If a lien is redeemed, the investor can earn a return based on these interest rates, which can range from 4% to 36% or more, depending on the state.

Another reward is the possibility of acquiring real estate at a fraction of its market value. If a lien is not redeemed within the redemption period, the investor has the right to foreclose on the property, potentially acquiring it for the amount of the unpaid taxes. This can represent a significant discount on the property's market value.

However, it's important to note that most tax liens are redeemed, and the opportunity to acquire properties through foreclosure is relatively rare. The primary return for most tax lien investors comes from the interest earned when liens are redeemed.

Now, let's turn to the risks. One of the primary risks is that the lien may not be redeemed. While most property owners do redeem their liens to avoid losing their property, there are cases where this does not happen. If the property is worthless or has significant liabilities, such as environmental contamination, the owner may choose to let it go. In such cases, the investor may be left with a property that is worth less than the amount they invested.

Another risk is related to the foreclosure process. Foreclosing on a property can be a complex, time-consuming, and costly process. It may involve legal fees, court costs, and other expenses. If the property's value does not exceed these costs, the investor may end up losing money.

There's also the risk of errors or omissions in the tax lien sale process. If the county or municipality did not follow all the required procedures in conducting the tax lien sale, the sale could be invalidated. This could result in the investor losing their investment.

Finally, there's the risk associated with the property itself. The investor does not have the opportunity to inspect the property before purchasing the tax lien certificate. There may be issues with the property that affect its value, such as structural problems, zoning restrictions, or other liens.

Investing in tax lien certificates offers the potential for high returns and the possibility of acquiring real estate at a discount. However, it also comes with significant risks, including the possibility that the lien will not be redeemed, the costs and complexities of foreclosure, potential errors in the tax lien sale process, and issues with the property itself. As with any investment, it's important to thoroughly research and understand these risks and rewards before diving in. With careful due diligence and a clear understanding of the process, tax lien investing can be a profitable addition to an investment portfolio.

Chapter 5

THE STATES THAT SELL TAX LIENS

1. An Overview of Tax Lien States

In the United States, tax lien investing is governed by state laws, which means that the rules and procedures can vary greatly from one state to another. It's crucial for investors to understand these differences and to be aware of which states sell tax liens.

There are currently about 30 states, plus the District of Columbia, that sell tax liens. These states are spread across the country, from Florida and Georgia in the South, to Colorado and Arizona in the West, to New Jersey and Maryland in the East. Each of these states has its own unique set of laws and regulations governing tax lien sales, which can affect everything from the bidding process to the rate of return to the redemption period.

In a tax lien state, when a property owner fails to pay their property taxes, the county government will sell a tax lien certificate to an investor. The investor then has the right to collect the unpaid taxes, plus interest, from the property owner. If the property owner fails to pay within the redemption period, the investor can potentially foreclose on the property.

The interest rates on tax liens can be quite attractive, often much higher than traditional investments. The rates are set by state law and can range from 5% to 36% per year, depending on the state. Some states use a bidding system where the interest rate is bid down, while others use a premium bidding system where the amount of the lien is bid up.

The redemption period, which is the time the property owner has to pay off the lien, also varies by state. It can be as short as six months or as long as three years. Some states offer a right of redemption even after foreclosure, giving the property owner one last chance to pay off the lien and keep their property.

It's also worth noting that in some states, tax liens have a higher priority than other liens, such as mortgages. This means that if the property is foreclosed, the tax lien holder gets paid before other creditors.

Understanding these nuances is crucial for investors, as it can greatly impact the potential return on investment and the overall strategy. For example, a state with a high interest rate might be attractive for its potential returns, but if the redemption period is long and the property owner has a post-foreclosure right of redemption, the risk might be higher.

Tax lien investing offers a unique opportunity for investors to earn attractive returns while helping local governments collect unpaid taxes. However, it's a complex field governed by a myriad of state laws. As such, it's crucial for investors to understand the landscape of tax lien states and to carefully research the laws and procedures of each state before investing. As always, it's advisable to consult with a financial advisor or investment professional to ensure you're making sound investment decisions.

2. How Each State Differs (the most up-to-date and recent information possible)

As we navigate through the realm of tax lien investing, it's important to understand that not all states are created equal in this regard. Each state has its own laws and procedures for selling tax liens, and these differences can have a significant impact on your investment strategy.

In some states, tax lien sales are quite straightforward. The state publishes a list of properties with unpaid taxes, holds an auction, and sells the tax lien to the highest bidder. The investor then earns interest on the lien until it's redeemed. These states often have high maximum interest rates, making them attractive to investors. Examples of such states include Arizona, Colorado, and Illinois.

Other states use a bid-down process, where the interest rate starts at a maximum level and is bid down during the auction. The lien goes to the bidder willing to accept the lowest interest rate. While this can result in lower returns, it also often means less competition and more opportunities for investors. Examples of bid-down states include Florida and New Jersey.

Some states use a premium bidding process, where the bidding starts at the amount of the unpaid taxes and goes up from there. The winning bidder pays the bid amount to the county and receives a tax lien certificate with a face value equal to the unpaid taxes, earning interest on this amount. However, the premium paid above the amount of the unpaid taxes does not earn interest. This process can result in lower effective interest rates, especially in competitive auctions. Examples of premium bidding states include Indiana and Iowa.

Then there are states like Texas and Georgia, which sell tax deeds rather than tax liens. In these states, the county sells the property itself, rather than just the unpaid taxes. The winning bidder becomes the property owner, subject to the former owner's right of redemption. These states can offer opportunities to acquire properties at a discount, but they also involve more risk and complexity.

It's also worth noting that some states don't sell tax liens at all. In these states, the county handles the collection of unpaid taxes directly, without involving investors. Examples of such states include North Carolina and Kentucky.

Each state has its own approach to selling tax liens, and these differences can significantly impact your investment strategy. Some states offer high interest rates, some use a bid-down or premium bidding process, and some sell tax deeds rather than tax liens. Understanding these differences is crucial for choosing where to invest and for tailoring your bidding strategy to the specific dynamics of each state's tax lien sales. As always, thorough research and due diligence are key to navigating these complexities and achieving success in the world of tax lien investing.

3. Best States for Beginners

As a beginner in the realm of tax lien investing, you might be wondering where to start. While each state has its own unique characteristics and procedures, some states are particularly well-suited for those new to this type of investment. These states offer a combination of investor-friendly laws, accessible information, and robust markets that make them ideal starting points.

One such state is Arizona. Known for its high interest rates of 16% and its large volume of tax lien sales, Arizona offers a wealth of opportunities for investors. The state provides comprehensive online resources, including lists of properties with unpaid taxes and details about upcoming auctions. This makes it easy for beginners to research potential investments and understand the process.

Florida is another state that is well-suited for beginners. It uses a bid-down process, where the interest rate starts at 18% and is bid down during the auction. This can result in lower returns, but it also often means less competition and more opportunities for investors. Florida also has a large volume of tax lien sales and provides extensive online resources.

Colorado is another great state for beginners. It offers an interest rate of 9% plus the federal discount rate, making it one of the highest in the country. Colorado also has a relatively straightforward process for tax lien sales, with detailed information available online.

Indiana is a good choice for those who are interested in premium bidding. The state offers a high interest rate of 10% per six months for the first year, and its premium bidding process can result in lower effective interest rates, especially in competitive auctions. Indiana also provides extensive online resources, making it easy for beginners to get started.

Finally, Maryland is worth considering for beginners. It offers an interest rate of up to 24% and uses a bid-down process. Maryland also has a relatively short redemption period of six months for residential properties, which can result in quicker returns.

While each state has its own unique characteristics and procedures, states like Arizona, Florida, Colorado, Indiana, and Maryland offer a combination of high interest rates, accessible information, and robust markets that make them ideal for beginners. However, it's important to remember that success in tax lien investing requires thorough research and due diligence. Always take the time to understand the laws and procedures in the state where you're investing, research potential investments carefully, and consider seeking advice from experienced investors or professionals. With the right approach, tax lien investing can be a profitable venture, even for beginners.

4. How to Participate in Out-of-State Auctions

As we continue our exploration of tax lien investing, it's important to recognize that you're not limited to purchasing tax liens in your home state. In fact, participating in out-of-state auctions can open up a world of opportunities, giving you access to markets with higher interest rates, more available liens, or more favorable laws. However, investing in out-of-state tax liens also comes with its own set of challenges and considerations.

The first step in participating in out-of-state auctions is research. You'll need to familiarize yourself with the laws and procedures of the state where you're considering investing. This includes understanding the interest rates, the bidding process, the redemption period, and the foreclosure process. You'll also need to find out when and where auctions are held, and what the requirements are for participation. Many counties provide this information on their websites, or you can contact the county tax collector's office directly.

Once you've done your research, the next step is to register for the auction. This often involves filling out a form and paying a deposit, which is usually refundable. Some counties require you to register in person, while others allow online registration. Be sure to register well in advance of the auction, as some counties have deadlines for registration.

In terms of actually participating in the auction, many counties now offer online auctions, which are accessible to investors anywhere. These online auctions work much like traditional in-person auctions, with liens going to the highest bidder. You'll need to set up an account with the auction platform, and you may need to pay a deposit or provide a letter of credit.

If the auction is in person, you'll need to travel to the location of the auction. This can add to the cost of your investment, so be sure to factor travel expenses into your calculations when determining your bidding strategy.

When bidding at the auction, whether online or in person, it's important to stick to your budget and not get caught up in the heat of the moment. Remember, the goal is to purchase liens at a price that allows for a good return on investment.

After the auction, you'll need to pay for any liens you've won. The payment process varies by county, but it usually involves sending a cashier's check or wire transfer. Once you've paid, the county will issue you a tax lien certificate.

Finally, remember that investing in out-of-state tax liens involves ongoing responsibilities. You'll need to track the redemption period, pay any subsequent taxes that become due, and potentially handle the foreclosure process if the lien isn't redeemed. All of this can be more challenging when dealing with properties and government offices in another state.

Participating in out-of-state auctions can offer exciting opportunities for tax lien investors. However, it requires careful research, preparation, and ongoing management. By understanding the laws and procedures of the state where you're investing, registering for the auction, bidding wisely, and managing your investment diligently, you can expand your investment horizons and potentially achieve higher returns.

5. Building a Multi-State Portfolio

Building a multi-state portfolio can be a strategic move in the realm of tax lien investing. By diversifying across different states, you can potentially access higher returns, mitigate risks, and take advantage of unique opportunities in different markets. However, managing a multi-state portfolio also comes with its own set of challenges.

The first step in building a multi-state portfolio is research. Each state has its own laws, interest rates, and market dynamics, so it's crucial to understand these factors before investing. Look for states that offer high interest rates, robust tax lien markets, and investor-friendly laws. Also consider the state's economic conditions, as these can affect property values and the likelihood of liens being redeemed.

Once you've identified potential states, the next step is to participate in auctions. This may involve traveling to in-person auctions or participating in online auctions. Be prepared to register for each auction, pay deposits, and meet any other requirements.

When bidding, be strategic. Diversification is a key advantage of a multi-state portfolio, so aim to purchase a mix of liens with different interest rates, redemption periods, and property types. Also, consider the total amount of your investment in each state. Investing too heavily in one state could expose you to more risk if that state's market experiences a downturn.

Managing a multi-state portfolio requires organization. You'll need to track the redemption periods for each lien, pay any subsequent taxes, and potentially handle foreclosures. This can be more complex with a multi-state portfolio, as you'll need to navigate the laws and procedures of multiple states.

Finally, consider seeking professional help. Tax lien investing can be complex, and managing a multi-state portfolio adds an additional layer of complexity. A lawyer or investment advisor experienced in tax lien investing can provide valuable guidance and help you avoid potential pitfalls.

Building a multi-state portfolio can be a profitable strategy in tax lien investing. By diversifying across different states, you can potentially achieve higher returns and mitigate risks. However, it requires careful research, strategic bidding, diligent management, and potentially professional help. With the right approach, a multi-state portfolio can be a valuable addition to your investment strategy.

Chapter 6

TAX DEED INVESTING AND PROFITS

1. What Happens After Acquiring a Deed

As we shift our focus to tax deed investing, it's important to understand what happens after acquiring a deed. When you purchase a tax deed, you're buying the property itself, not just a lien on the property. This means that once you acquire the deed, you become the owner of the property. This ownership, however, comes with a set of responsibilities and opportunities that you need to navigate carefully.

The first thing you need to do after acquiring a deed is to confirm your ownership. This typically involves recording the deed with the county recorder's office. The exact process varies by county, but it usually involves submitting the deed and paying a recording fee. Once the deed is recorded, you're officially the owner of the property.

The next step is to assess the property. Since tax deed sales often don't allow for a thorough inspection before the auction, this may be your first chance to evaluate the property in detail. You'll want to assess the condition of the property, identify any necessary repairs or renovations, and determine the property's market value. This assessment will help inform your strategy for the property, whether that's to renovate, rent, or sell.

It's also crucial to address any issues with the property as soon as possible. This might include cleaning up the property, securing it against vandalism, addressing any code violations, or starting on necessary repairs. Remember, as the property owner, you're responsible for the property's condition and any associated liabilities.

Another important step is to ensure the property is insured. This protects your investment against damage or loss. It's a good idea to arrange for insurance as soon as you acquire the deed, as there may be a waiting period before coverage takes effect.

Finally, you'll want to consider your tax obligations. As the property owner, you're responsible for paying property taxes. You'll also need to consider the tax implications of your strategy for the property, whether that's selling, renting, or holding the property for long-term gains.

Acquiring a tax deed is just the first step in tax deed investing. Once you own the deed, you need to confirm your ownership, assess the property, address any issues, ensure the property is insured, and consider your tax obligations. These steps lay the groundwork for your strategy for the property, setting you up for success in your tax deed investment.

2. Renovation or Sale?

Once you've acquired a tax deed and assessed the property, you're faced with a critical decision: should you renovate the property or sell it as is? This decision will largely depend on your assessment of the property, your resources, and your overall investment strategy.

If the property is in good condition and located in a desirable market, selling it as is could be a viable option. This approach allows you to recoup your investment quickly, potentially at a profit. However, keep in mind that selling a property involves costs, including real estate commissions and closing costs. You'll also need to consider the tax implications of a sale, as any profit will likely be subject to capital gains tax.

On the other hand, if the property requires significant repairs or is located in a less desirable market, renovating it could increase its value and make it more appealing to potential buyers. Renovations could range from minor cosmetic updates to major structural repairs. The goal is to increase the property's market value, enabling you to sell it at a higher price.

However, renovations come with their own set of challenges. They can be costly and time-consuming, and there's always the risk of unforeseen issues or cost overruns. You'll also need to consider the cost of carrying the property while the renovations are being done, including property taxes, insurance, and any financing costs.

When deciding between renovation or sale, it's important to do a thorough cost-benefit analysis. Estimate the potential sale price of the property in its current condition and after renovations. Then, subtract the costs associated with each option, including renovation costs, selling costs, carrying costs, and taxes. This will give you a rough estimate of the potential profit under each scenario.

It's also important to consider your own skills, resources, and preferences. If you have experience in home renovations, a network of reliable contractors, or access to low-cost financing, renovating may be a more viable option. On the other hand, if you're looking for a quick return on your investment and prefer not to deal with the complexities of a renovation project, selling as is might be the better choice.

Finally, keep in mind that there's no one-size-fits-all answer to this question. The best choice depends on the specifics of the property, the local real estate market, and your own situation and goals. Whether you choose to renovate or sell, the key is to make an informed decision based on careful analysis and sound judgment.

The decision to renovate or sell a property acquired through a tax deed sale is a critical one. By carefully assessing the property, estimating costs and potential profits, considering your own resources and preferences, and making an informed decision, you can maximize your return on investment and achieve success in tax deed investing.

3. Flipping Tax Deed Properties

Flipping tax deed properties is a strategy that involves buying a property at a tax deed sale, renovating it, and then selling it for a profit. This approach can be lucrative, but it also involves significant risks and requires careful planning and execution.

The first step in flipping a tax deed property is to acquire the property at a tax deed sale. As we've discussed, this involves researching potential properties, participating in the auction, and successfully bidding on a property. When choosing a property to flip, look for properties that are undervalued due to their condition or other factors, but that have potential for improvement.

Once you've acquired the property, the next step is to plan and execute the renovation. This involves assessing the property's condition, determining what repairs and improvements are needed, and estimating the cost of these renovations. You'll also need to consider the time frame for the renovation, as carrying costs can add up the longer the project takes.

The renovation process itself can be complex and challenging. It often involves coordinating with contractors, obtaining permits, and managing unexpected issues that arise. It's crucial to stay on top of the project, ensuring that work is completed on time and on budget.

Once the renovation is complete, the next step is to sell the property. This involves marketing the property, negotiating with potential buyers, and navigating the closing process. Keep in mind that selling a property can take time, and there are costs associated with the sale, including real estate commissions and closing costs.

Flipping tax deed properties can be profitable, but it's not without risks. The property may require more extensive repairs than anticipated, the renovation may take longer than planned, or the property may not sell for as much as expected. It's also a strategy that requires significant capital, as you'll need to cover the cost of the property, the renovations, and the carrying costs until the property is sold.

To mitigate these risks, it's important to do thorough due diligence before buying a property to flip. This includes researching the property and the local real estate market, estimating renovation costs accurately, and having a realistic idea of the potential sale price. It's also a good idea to have a contingency plan in case the project doesn't go as planned.

It's also worth considering working with a partner or seeking financing to help cover the costs of flipping a property. This can reduce your financial risk and provide additional resources for the project.

Flipping tax deed properties is a strategy that can offer significant profits, but it also involves substantial risks and requires careful planning and execution. By doing thorough due diligence, managing the renovation process effectively, and navigating the sale process skillfully, you can maximize your chances of success in flipping tax deed properties.

4. Holding for Long-Term Gains

While flipping tax deed properties can provide quick profits, another strategy to consider is holding properties for long-term gains. This approach involves buying a property at a tax deed sale, possibly making some renovations or improvements, and then holding onto the property for several years to benefit from appreciation and rental income.

One of the main advantages of this strategy is the potential for steady, passive income. If the property is in a condition to be rented out, you can start earning rental income almost immediately. This can provide a steady cash flow while you wait for the property to appreciate in value.

Another advantage is the potential for significant appreciation. Real estate generally tends to appreciate over time, although the rate of appreciation can vary greatly depending on the location and the state of the real estate market. By holding onto a property for several years, you can potentially benefit from this appreciation and sell the property for significantly more than you paid for it.

Holding a property for the long term also allows for more flexibility. If the real estate market is down when you acquire the property, you have the option to wait it out and sell when the market improves. Similarly, if the rental market is strong, you can benefit from rental income until you're ready to sell.

However, holding properties for long-term gains also comes with its own set of challenges. One of the main challenges is the ongoing costs associated with owning a property. This includes property taxes, insurance, maintenance costs, and potentially property management fees if you choose to hire a property manager. You'll need to ensure that the rental income you receive is sufficient to cover these costs.

Another challenge is dealing with tenants. If you choose to rent out the property, you'll need to find and manage tenants, handle repairs and maintenance, and deal with any issues that arise. This can be time-consuming and stressful, especially if you own multiple properties.

Finally, holding a property for the long term involves more uncertainty than flipping. The real estate market can be unpredictable, and there's no guarantee that the property will appreciate as expected. You'll also need to be prepared for potential vacancies, unexpected maintenance costs, and other risks associated with owning rental property.

Holding tax deed properties for long-term gains is a strategy that can provide steady income and significant appreciation. However, it involves ongoing costs, the challenges of managing rental property, and the uncertainty of the real estate market. By carefully selecting properties, managing them effectively, and being prepared for the risks, you can achieve success with this strategy.

5. Success Stories

As we delve into the world of tax deed investing, it can be inspiring and educational to learn from the success stories of those who have navigated this path before us. These stories provide valuable insights into the strategies, challenges, and rewards of tax deed investing.

Consider the story of John, a small business owner who turned to tax deed investing as a way to diversify his income. John started by researching tax deed sales in his home state of Florida. He attended several auctions, gradually learning the ropes and bidding on properties. His first purchase was a small residential property, which he was able to rent out for a steady income. Over the years, John has built a portfolio of rental properties purchased through tax deed sales, providing him with a significant passive income.

Then there's the story of Maria, a retired teacher who used tax deed investing as a way to supplement her retirement income. Maria focused on her home state of Arizona, where she purchased tax deeds and then sold the properties for a profit. Maria's strategy was to look for properties in desirable locations that were undervalued due to their condition. She would then make minor cosmetic improvements to increase the property's appeal and market value. This strategy allowed Maria to earn a substantial profit on each property she sold.

Another inspiring story is that of David, a real estate investor who used tax deed investing to expand his portfolio. David focused on states with high interest rates and robust tax deed markets, such as Texas and Georgia. He would buy properties at tax deed sales, renovate them, and then flip them for a profit. Over time, David was able to build a successful business flipping tax deed properties.

Finally, consider the story of Lisa, a young professional who used tax deed investing as a way to break into the real estate market. Lisa started by attending tax deed sales in her home state of Colorado. She purchased a small condo at a tax deed sale, renovated it, and then sold it for a substantial profit. This initial success gave Lisa the confidence and capital to continue investing in tax deed properties.

These success stories illustrate the potential of tax deed investing. Whether it's building a portfolio of rental properties, flipping properties for a profit, or breaking into the real estate market, tax deed investing offers a range of opportunities. However, these stories also highlight the importance of research, due diligence, and a well-planned strategy. By learning from the successes of others, you can navigate the world of tax deed investing and create your own success story.

Chapter 7

AVOIDING COMMON PITFALLS

1. The Most Common Mistakes Investors Make

Investing in tax liens and deeds can be a rewarding venture, but like any investment, it comes with its share of potential pitfalls. By understanding the most common mistakes investors make, you can avoid these missteps and increase your chances of success.

One of the most common mistakes is failing to do adequate research. Each state has its own laws and procedures for tax lien and deed sales, and it's crucial to understand these before you start bidding. This includes understanding the bidding process, the redemption period, the interest rate, and any penalties or fees. Failing to understand these details can lead to costly mistakes.

Another common mistake is not conducting thorough due diligence on the properties. Before bidding on a tax lien or deed, it's important to research the property. This includes checking the property's condition, its market value, and any liens or encumbrances. Neglecting this step can result in purchasing a property that requires costly repairs or has other issues that diminish its value.

Overbidding is another common mistake. In the heat of an auction, it can be easy to get caught up and bid more than a property is worth. This can result in a lower return on your investment, or even a loss. It's important to set a maximum bid based on your research and stick to it.

Neglecting to monitor the investment is another mistake that can be costly. If you've purchased a tax lien, you need to track the redemption period and be ready to foreclose if the lien isn't redeemed. If you've purchased a tax deed, you need to record the deed, maintain the property, and pay any subsequent taxes. Failing to manage these responsibilities can lead to penalties, additional costs, or even loss of the property.

Finally, many investors make the mistake of not seeking professional advice. Tax lien and deed investing can be complex, and it's often beneficial to work with a lawyer or investment advisor. Professionals can help you navigate the legal and logistical complexities, avoid potential pitfalls, and make informed decisions.

While tax lien and deed investing offers significant opportunities, it's not without risks. By avoiding common mistakes - such as failing to do adequate research, not conducting thorough due diligence, overbidding, neglecting to monitor the investment, and not seeking professional advice - you can increase your chances of success and make the most of your investment. Remember, every investor makes mistakes, but the key is to learn from these mistakes and continuously improve your strategy.

2. How to Conduct Thorough Due Diligence

Due diligence is a critical aspect of tax lien and deed investing. It involves thoroughly researching and assessing a property before bidding on it at a tax sale. Proper due diligence can help you avoid costly mistakes and increase your chances of a successful investment.

The first step in conducting due diligence is to gather as much information as possible about the property. This includes the property's location, size, condition, and market value. You can often find this information through online real estate databases, county property records, and physical inspections.

Next, check the property's title. This involves looking for any liens or encumbrances on the property, such as mortgages, judgments, or unpaid taxes. These can affect the property's value and your ability to take possession of the property if you're buying a tax lien. You can check the property's title through a title search, which can be done online or through a title company.

It's also important to understand the local real estate market. Look at recent sales of comparable properties in the area to get an idea of the property's market value. Also consider factors like the local economy, the rental market, and future development plans for the area. These can affect the property's value and your potential return on investment.

If you're considering bidding on a tax lien, you'll also want to understand the redemption process. This includes the redemption period, the interest rate, and any penalties or fees. You'll need to factor these into your investment strategy and be prepared to foreclose on the property if the lien isn't redeemed.

Finally, consider seeking professional advice. A lawyer or investment advisor can provide valuable guidance, help you navigate the complexities of tax lien and deed investing, and ensure that you're making informed decisions.

Conducting thorough due diligence is a critical step in tax lien and deed investing. By gathering information about the property, checking the title, understanding the local real estate market, and understanding the redemption process, you can make informed decisions and increase your chances of a successful investment. And remember, while due diligence can take time and effort, it's a crucial investment in your success.

3. Recognizing Red Flags

As you navigate the path of tax lien and deed investing, it's crucial to be vigilant and recognize potential red flags. These warning signs could indicate problems that could undermine your investment or signal that a particular property or sale might not be the right fit for your portfolio.

One red flag is a property with multiple tax liens. While a single tax lien can provide an investment opportunity, multiple liens can complicate the process and increase the risk. The presence of multiple liens could indicate serious financial distress, which might make it less likely that the property owner will be able to redeem the lien. It could also mean that you'll have to navigate a more complex process to take possession of the property.

Another red flag is a property in severe disrepair. While it's common for properties at tax sales to need some work, a property in poor condition could require costly repairs that could eat into your profits. If you're not prepared to take on a major renovation project, such a property might not be the best choice for your investment.

A property in a declining neighborhood or area with a weak real estate market is another potential red flag. Even if the property itself is in good condition, if it's in an area where property values are falling or where there's a high vacancy rate, it could be difficult to sell or rent the property for a profit.

The absence of clear property records is another red flag. Before bidding on a tax lien or deed, you should be able to review the property's title and tax records. If these records are incomplete or unclear, it could indicate potential issues with the property's ownership or tax status.

If you're considering a tax lien investment, a low interest rate could be a red flag. While a lower rate might seem attractive, it could also indicate a higher risk. In some cases, jurisdictions may offer lower rates on liens for properties that are considered less desirable or more risky.

Finally, be wary of any tax sale or investment opportunity that seems too good to be true. If a property is being sold for a significantly lower price than its apparent market value, or if a tax lien is offering an unusually high rate of return, there may be hidden risks or issues that you're not aware of.

Recognizing red flags is an essential part of successful tax lien and deed investing. By being vigilant and cautious, you can avoid potential pitfalls and make more informed investment decisions.

Remember, every investment carries some risk, but by recognizing and understanding these red flags, you can manage and mitigate these risks.

4. Working with Professionals

While tax lien and deed investing can be a profitable venture, it can also be complex and fraught with potential pitfalls. One way to navigate these complexities and mitigate risks is to work with professionals. These could include real estate agents, attorneys, tax advisors, and property managers, among others.

Real estate agents can provide valuable assistance in understanding the local real estate market, assessing the value of properties, and selling properties once you're ready to exit your investment. They can provide insights into market trends, help you determine a fair price for a property, and connect you with potential buyers or renters.

Attorneys, particularly those specializing in real estate or tax law, can help you navigate the legal complexities of tax lien and deed investing. They can help you understand the laws and regulations in your state, assist with the foreclosure process if necessary, and help you avoid potential legal pitfalls. While hiring an attorney can add to your investment costs, it can also save you from costly legal mistakes.

Tax advisors can provide guidance on the tax implications of your investments. This can include advice on how to structure your investments for tax efficiency, guidance on the tax implications of selling properties or earning rental income, and assistance with tax planning and filing. A tax advisor can help you understand and minimize your tax liability, maximizing your after-tax return on investment.

Property managers can be invaluable if you're investing in rental properties. They can handle the day-to-day management of the property, including finding and screening tenants, collecting rent, handling repairs and maintenance, and dealing with any issues that arise. While property management comes at a cost, it can also free up your time and reduce the stress of managing rental properties.

Working with professionals can provide several benefits. It can save you time, reduce your risk, and potentially increase your return on investment. However, it's important to choose your professionals carefully. Look for individuals or firms with experience in tax lien and deed investing, a strong reputation, and a commitment to client service.

Keep in mind that while professionals can provide valuable assistance, they can't eliminate all risks. You'll still need to do your own due diligence, make your own investment decisions, and monitor your investments. Working with professionals should be seen as a complement to, not a substitute for, your own efforts.

Working with professionals can be a valuable strategy for navigating the complexities and mitigating the risks of tax lien and deed investing. By choosing your professionals wisely and using their services effectively, you can increase your chances of success in this potentially lucrative investment arena.

5. Learning from Failure

In the world of tax lien and deed investing, as in any investment venture, failure is a possibility. You might purchase a property that doesn't yield the expected returns, encounter unforeseen complications, or face market downturns that impact your investments. But while these setbacks can be disheartening, they also provide invaluable opportunities for learning and growth.

When you face a setback in your investing journey, the first step is to take a step back and assess what went wrong. Was there a flaw in your due diligence process? Did you misjudge the market conditions? Did you overextend your resources? By identifying the factors that contributed to the failure, you can gain insights into what needs to change in your approach.

Once you've identified the factors that led to the failure, the next step is to develop a plan for addressing these issues. This might involve refining your due diligence process, seeking additional education or advice, or adjusting your investment strategy. The goal is to turn the failure into a learning experience that strengthens your investing skills and strategies.

It's also important to maintain a balanced perspective. While it's essential to learn from failure, it's equally important not to let failure deter you from pursuing your investment goals. Remember, even the most successful investors have faced setbacks. What sets them apart is their ability to learn from these experiences and persist in their efforts.

Finally, don't hesitate to seek support. This can come from a mentor, a professional advisor, or a network of fellow investors. Others can offer valuable insights, advice, and encouragement to help you navigate the challenges and come out stronger on the other side.

While failure can be a difficult part of the investment journey, it can also be a powerful catalyst for learning and growth. By assessing what went wrong, developing a plan for improvement, maintaining a balanced perspective, and seeking support, you can turn failure into a stepping stone on the path to investment success. Remember, the road to success is often paved with lessons learned from failure.

Chapter 8

FINANCING YOUR INVESTMENTS

1. Using Investor Funds

Investor funds can be a valuable resource for financing your tax lien and deed investments. This involves raising capital from other individuals or entities who are interested in sharing in the potential returns from your investment activities. There are several ways to approach this, each with its own advantages and considerations.

One common approach is to form a partnership or joint venture with one or more investors. In this arrangement, each partner contributes capital to the venture and shares in the profits and losses. This can be an effective way to pool resources and share risks, but it also requires careful management to ensure that all partners' interests are protected.

Another approach is to raise funds from private investors. This can be done through a private placement, which is a type of securities offering that is not registered with the Securities and Exchange Commission. Private placements can provide a flexible and efficient way to raise capital, but they also come with regulatory requirements and potential legal risks.

Crowdfunding is another option for raising investor funds. This involves soliciting small investments from a large number of individuals, typically through an online platform. Real estate crowdfunding has become increasingly popular in recent years, thanks to changes in securities laws that have made it more accessible. However, it also requires careful planning and management, and it's subject to regulatory oversight.

When using investor funds, it's important to be transparent and ethical in your dealings with investors. This includes providing accurate and complete information about the investment opportunity, using the funds as promised, and providing regular updates on the investment's performance.

It's also important to understand the legal and regulatory implications of raising investor funds. Depending on how you structure the investment and who you raise funds from, you may be subject to securities laws and other regulations. It's often advisable to work with a lawyer or other professional advisor when raising investor funds.

Using investor funds can be an effective way to finance your tax lien and deed investments. Whether through partnerships, private placements, or crowdfunding, investor funds can provide the capital you need to pursue investment opportunities. However, raising investor funds requires careful planning, transparent communication, and compliance with legal and regulatory requirements. By navigating these considerations effectively, you can leverage investor funds to expand your investment activities and increase your potential returns.

2. Self-Funding Your Investment

Self-funding your investment is another viable option in the realm of tax lien and deed investing. This approach involves using your own personal funds to finance your investments, rather than relying on external sources like loans or investor funds. While this method may seem straightforward, it requires careful planning and consideration.

One of the key advantages of self-funding is the level of control it provides. When you finance your investments with your own funds, you have complete control over your investment decisions. You're not beholden to the expectations or demands of lenders or investors, which can give you more freedom and flexibility in your investment strategy.

Another advantage of self-funding is that it allows you to retain all the profits from your investments. Unlike with investor funds or loans, there's no need to share your returns or pay interest. This can potentially lead to higher net returns, assuming your investments are successful.

However, self-funding also comes with risks. One of the main risks is the potential for loss. If your investments don't perform as expected, you could lose some or all of your invested capital. This risk can be mitigated through careful due diligence and a diversified investment strategy, but it cannot be eliminated entirely.

Another consideration is the opportunity cost. When you use your own funds for investing, those funds are not available for other uses. You'll need to consider whether the potential returns from tax lien and deed investing outweigh the potential returns from other uses of your funds.

Finally, self-funding may limit the scale of your investments. Depending on your financial resources, you may not be able to finance as many or as large investments as you could with external financing. This could limit your potential returns, although it could also limit your potential losses.

Self-funding can be an effective way to finance your tax lien and deed investments, providing control, the potential for higher net returns, and the freedom to pursue your own investment strategy. However, it also comes with risks and limitations, including the potential for loss, opportunity cost, and limits on the scale of your investments. By carefully considering these factors and planning your investment strategy accordingly, you can make the most of self-funding as a financing option.

3. Loans and Lines of Credit (the most up-to-date and recent information possible)

5444Loans and lines of credit represent another financing option for your tax lien and deed investments. These financial instruments can provide the necessary capital to make investments, particularly for larger or more expensive properties that may be beyond your immediate personal resources.

Loans, such as personal loans or business loans, provide a lump sum of money that you repay over time with interest. These can be obtained from banks, credit unions, or online lenders. The interest rate and terms of the loan will depend on your creditworthiness and other factors. For tax lien and deed investing, a key advantage of loans is that they provide a large sum of money upfront, which can be used to finance substantial investments.

Lines of credit, on the other hand, provide a flexible source of funding. A line of credit is a preset amount of money that you can borrow from as needed. You only pay interest on the amount you've borrowed, and you can repay and borrow from the line of credit repeatedly as long as you don't exceed the credit limit. This can be particularly useful for tax lien and deed investing, where the cost of investments can vary and the need for funds can arise unexpectedly.

In recent years, lenders have become increasingly open to providing loans and lines of credit for real estate investing, including tax lien and deed investing. However, these financial products are not without risks. If your investments don't yield the expected returns, you could struggle to repay the loan or line of credit, which could harm your credit and potentially lead to legal action from the lender.

It's also important to consider the cost of borrowing. Loans and lines of credit come with interest and often fees, which can eat into your investment returns. You'll need to factor these costs into your investment calculations to ensure that the potential returns from your investments outweigh the costs of borrowing.

Finally, keep in mind that lenders will typically require a credit check and may require collateral or a personal guarantee. This can put your personal assets at risk if you're unable to repay the loan or line of credit.

Loans and lines of credit can provide valuable financing for tax lien and deed investments, particularly for larger investments or for investors with limited personal resources. However, they also come with risks and costs, and require careful consideration and management. By understanding these factors and using loans and lines of credit wisely, you can leverage these financial tools to expand your investment opportunities and increase your potential returns.

4. Leveraging Equity from Other Properties

Leveraging equity from other properties is a strategic way to finance your tax lien and deed investments. This approach involves using the equity you've built up in one property to fund investments in other properties. It's a method often used by seasoned real estate investors, but it's also accessible to beginners with a property that has accumulated significant equity.

Equity is the difference between the current market value of your property and the amount you owe on any mortgages or loans secured by the property. As you pay down your mortgage and as the value of your property increases, your equity grows. This equity can be tapped into through a home equity loan or a home equity line of credit (HELOC).

A home equity loan is a second mortgage that allows you to borrow a lump sum of money based on the equity in your property. It's repaid over a fixed period, much like your primary mortgage. The interest rates for home equity loans are typically lower than those for personal loans or credit cards, making it an attractive option for financing investments.

A HELOC, on the other hand, works more like a credit card. It provides a line of credit based on your home equity, which you can draw from as needed. You only pay interest on the amount you've borrowed, and you can borrow and repay funds repeatedly during the draw period. This flexibility makes a HELOC particularly useful for tax lien and deed investing, where the cost of investments can vary.

Leveraging equity from other properties allows you to make larger or more numerous investments than you might otherwise be able to afford. However, it's important to remember that your property is the collateral for the loan or line of credit. If you're unable to repay the borrowed funds, you could risk losing the property.

Additionally, the amount you can borrow is limited by the amount of equity in your property. If property values decline, your equity—and thus your borrowing power—could also decrease. It's also worth noting that there are costs associated with home equity loans and HELOCs, including interest and fees, which need to be factored into your investment calculations.

Leveraging equity from other properties can be a powerful tool for financing your tax lien and deed investments. It allows you to tap into the value of your existing real estate assets to expand your investment portfolio. However, like all financing methods, it requires careful consideration and management to balance the potential benefits against the risks and costs. By understanding these factors and using property equity wisely, you can effectively finance your investments and enhance your potential returns.

5. The Power of Compound Growth

The power of compound growth is a fundamental concept in finance and investing, and it's particularly relevant when considering how to finance your tax lien and deed investments. Compound growth refers to the process where the returns on an investment are reinvested, leading to increasingly larger returns over time.

In the context of tax lien and deed investing, compound growth can occur when the returns from one investment are used to finance additional investments. For example, if you purchase a tax lien that yields a significant return, you could use that return to purchase additional liens. Over time, this can lead to a snowball effect, where your investments and returns grow increasingly larger.

The key to harnessing the power of compound growth is time. The longer your investments have to grow, the more significant the effects of compounding become. This underscores the importance of starting your investment journey as early as possible and maintaining a long-term perspective.

It's also important to reinvest your returns. While it can be tempting to spend the returns from your investments, reinvesting those returns allows you to benefit from compound growth. This doesn't mean you can't ever use your investment returns, but a focus on reinvestment can enhance your long-term growth potential.

One of the benefits of tax lien and deed investing is that it can provide relatively high returns, which can be particularly beneficial for compound growth. However, it's important to balance this potential for high returns against the risks and costs associated with these investments.

The power of compound growth is a powerful tool in your investment financing toolkit. By understanding and harnessing this power, you can enhance your ability to finance your investments and increase your potential returns. Remember, the key to compound growth is time and reinvestment. Start early, reinvest your returns, and let the power of compound growth work for you.

Chapter 9

TAX IMPLICATIONS AND PLANNING

1. Understanding Tax Laws (the most up-to-date and recent information possible)

Understanding tax laws is a crucial aspect of tax lien and deed investing. These laws can significantly impact your return on investment and the overall profitability of your investment strategy. Therefore, it's important to have a solid grasp of the tax implications before you dive into this type of investing.

Tax liens and deeds are, by their very nature, intertwined with the tax system. When a property owner fails to pay their property taxes, the government can place a tax lien on the property. Investors can then purchase these liens or the subsequent tax deeds, earning returns in the form of interest payments or ownership of the property.

The income you earn from tax lien and deed investing is generally subject to income tax. This can include interest earned from tax liens, rental income from properties acquired through tax deeds, and capital gains from selling these properties. The tax rates and rules can vary depending on your overall income, your location, and other factors.

One of the key tax considerations for tax lien and deed investors is the distinction between ordinary income and capital gains. Interest income from tax liens is typically considered ordinary income and is taxed at your regular income tax rate. However, if you acquire a property through a tax deed and later sell it, the profit may be considered a capital gain. Capital gains may be taxed at a lower rate than ordinary income, especially for long-term investments.

It's also important to be aware of any state-specific tax laws. Tax lien and deed investing is governed by state law, and the tax implications can vary from one state to another. Some states offer tax advantages for tax lien and deed investors, while others may impose additional taxes or fees.

Understanding tax laws is a critical part of tax lien and deed investing. These laws can significantly impact your returns, and failing to comply with them can result in penalties or other negative consequences. Therefore, it's advisable to research the tax laws related to tax lien and deed investing, both at the federal level and in the specific states where you plan to invest. It can also be beneficial to consult with a tax professional who can provide guidance tailored to your specific situation.

2. Tax Liens and Tax-Free Growth in IRAs

Investing in tax liens and deeds through a self-directed Individual Retirement Account (IRA) can offer significant tax advantages. IRAs are a type of retirement account that offer tax benefits to encourage long-term saving and investing. A self-directed IRA is a special type of IRA that allows for a wider range of investments, including real estate and tax liens.

When you invest in tax liens or deeds through a self-directed IRA, the income and gains from those investments can grow tax-free within the account. This means you won't owe taxes on the interest earned from tax liens or the profits from selling properties acquired through tax deeds, as long as the funds remain in the IRA. This can allow your investments to grow more quickly than they would in a taxable account.

There are two main types of IRAs that you might consider for tax lien and deed investing: Traditional IRAs and Roth IRAs. With a Traditional IRA, you may be able to deduct your contributions on your taxes, but you'll owe taxes when you withdraw the funds in retirement. With a Roth IRA, you contribute after-tax dollars, but qualified withdrawals in retirement are tax-free.

The tax-free growth in a Roth IRA can be particularly beneficial for tax lien and deed investing. Since you've already paid taxes on your contributions, you won't owe any taxes on the income or gains from your investments, even when you withdraw the funds in retirement. This can provide a significant boost to your long-term investment returns.

However, investing in tax liens and deeds through an IRA also comes with certain rules and restrictions. For example, you can't personally use any properties acquired through the IRA, and you can't conduct transactions with certain related parties. Also, any expenses related to the investments, such as property maintenance or lien redemption fees, must be paid from the IRA.

It's also worth noting that IRAs come with contribution limits, which can limit the amount you can invest each year. And while the funds in the IRA can grow tax-free, you could face penalties if you withdraw the funds before reaching the age of 59 and a half.

Investing in tax liens and deeds through a self-directed IRA can offer significant tax advantages, including tax-free growth and potentially tax-free withdrawals. However, it also comes with certain rules and restrictions that must be carefully followed. As always, it's advisable to consult with a tax professional or financial advisor to understand the tax implications and to ensure you're making the most of your investment strategy.

3. Handling Capital Gains

Capital gains are a significant aspect of tax lien and deed investing that need careful consideration. A capital gain occurs when you sell an asset for more than you paid for it. In the context of tax deed investing, if you acquire a property through a tax deed and later sell it for more than you paid, the profit is considered a capital gain.

The tax treatment of capital gains can significantly impact your overall return on investment. In the United States, capital gains are generally subject to capital gains tax. However, the rate at which these gains are taxed depends on several factors, including how long you held the asset before selling it.

If you sell an asset less than a year after acquiring it, the profit is considered a short-term capital gain and is typically taxed at your ordinary income tax rate. However, if you hold the asset for more than a year before selling it, the profit is considered a long-term capital gain and is usually taxed at a lower rate. For most taxpayers, the long-term capital gains tax rate is significantly lower than their ordinary income tax rate.

This distinction between short-term and long-term capital gains can have a significant impact on your tax liability and should be a key consideration in your investment strategy. In general, holding assets for more than a year before selling them can provide substantial tax savings.

However, it's also important to be aware of the potential for capital losses. If you sell an asset for less than you paid for it, the loss can offset other capital gains and reduce your overall tax liability. In some cases, you can even use capital losses to offset ordinary income.

Another important aspect of handling capital gains is record-keeping. It's essential to keep accurate records of your investments, including the purchase price, sale price, and any expenses related to the investment. These records will be crucial for calculating your capital gains or losses and for completing your tax return.

One more point to consider is the impact of state taxes. Some states also tax capital gains, often at the same rate as ordinary income. The rules and rates can vary by state, so it's important to understand the tax laws in the states where you invest.

Handling capital gains is a crucial part of tax lien and deed investing. The tax treatment of capital gains can significantly impact your returns, and understanding these rules can help you optimize your investment strategy. By holding assets for the long term, keeping accurate records, and understanding state tax laws, you can effectively manage your capital gains and enhance your investment returns. As always, it's advisable to consult with a tax professional to ensure you're handling your capital gains correctly and making the most of your investment strategy.

4. Tracking Your Investments for Tax Purposes

Tracking your investments for tax purposes is an essential part of tax lien and deed investing. Accurate and comprehensive record-keeping can make it easier to calculate your tax liability, prepare your tax return, and handle any potential audits or inquiries from the tax authorities.

One of the first steps in tracking your investments is to keep records of all your transactions. This includes the purchase and sale of tax liens or deeds, any interest or penalties received, and any expenses related to the investment. For each transaction, you should record the date, the amount, and any other relevant details.

In addition to transaction records, it's also important to keep documentation to support your records. This could include receipts, invoices, contracts, and any other documents that verify the details of the transaction. These documents can be crucial in the event of an audit or if any questions arise about your tax return.

Another key aspect of tracking your investments is calculating your basis in each investment. Your basis is the amount you've invested in a tax lien or deed, including the purchase price and any related expenses. This basis is used to calculate your capital gain or loss when you sell the investment. It's important to accurately calculate and record your basis for each investment.

If you're investing in tax liens or deeds through a self-directed IRA, you'll also need to track the flow of funds in and out of the IRA. This includes contributions to the IRA, distributions from the IRA, and any income or gains earned within the IRA. Keeping accurate records of these transactions can help ensure you comply with the rules for IRAs and avoid any potential penalties.

Tracking your investments can be a complex task, but there are tools and resources available to help. Many investors use spreadsheets or financial software to keep track of their transactions and calculate their gains or losses. There are also professional services that can handle this task for you, although these can be costly.

Tracking your investments for tax purposes is a crucial part of tax lien and deed investing. By keeping accurate records, supporting your records with documentation, and accurately calculating your basis, you can make your tax reporting easier and more accurate. While this task can be complex, it's an essential part of managing your investments and optimizing your returns. As always, it's advisable to consult with a tax professional to ensure you're tracking your investments correctly and complying with all relevant tax laws.

5. Working with a Tax Professional

Working with a tax professional can be a valuable part of your tax lien and deed investment strategy. Tax laws can be complex and change frequently, and a tax professional can provide the expertise and guidance needed to navigate these laws effectively.

A tax professional can help you understand the tax implications of your investments, including the treatment of interest income, capital gains, and potential deductions. They can also assist with tax planning, helping you structure your investments in a way that minimizes your tax liability and maximizes your after-tax returns.

For example, a tax professional can advise on the benefits and drawbacks of investing through a self-directed IRA, including the tax-free growth and potential penalties for early withdrawals. They can also help you understand the impact of state tax laws, which can vary widely and significantly affect your returns.

In addition to providing advice and planning, a tax professional can also assist with the practical aspects of handling your taxes. This can include preparing your tax return, calculating your capital gains or losses, and ensuring you comply with all relevant reporting requirements. If you're audited by the tax authorities, a tax professional can represent you and help resolve any issues.

When choosing a tax professional, it's important to look for someone with expertise in real estate and investment taxes. This is a specialized area of tax law, and not all tax professionals will have the necessary knowledge and experience. You may also want to consider whether the professional is a Certified Public Accountant (CPA) or an Enrolled Agent (EA), as these designations indicate a high level of expertise and professional standards.

Working with a tax professional can be a significant investment, but it can also provide significant benefits. By helping you understand and manage the tax implications of your investments, a tax professional can help you optimize your returns and avoid potential pitfalls.

A tax professional can be a valuable partner in your tax lien and deed investment journey. By providing expert advice, planning, and practical assistance, they can help you navigate the complex world of tax laws and maximize your after-tax returns. As always, it's important to choose a professional who is knowledgeable, experienced, and aligned with your investment goals and strategies.

Chapter 10

LONG-TERM SUCCESS STRATEGIES

1. Scaling Your Investment Portfolio

Scaling your investment portfolio is a key strategy for achieving long-term success in tax lien and deed investing. As you gain experience and confidence, and as your financial resources grow, you may want to consider increasing the size of your portfolio. This can involve investing in more tax liens or deeds, investing in higher-value properties, or both.

There are several advantages to scaling your investment portfolio. First, it can increase your potential returns. The more you invest, the more you can potentially earn in interest payments or profits from selling properties. Second, it can provide more opportunities for diversification, which can reduce risk. By investing in a variety of liens or deeds, you can spread your risk across multiple investments.

However, scaling your investment portfolio also comes with challenges. It requires more capital, more time and effort to manage the investments, and potentially more risk. Therefore, it's important to approach scaling in a strategic and measured way.

One approach to scaling is to reinvest your returns. As you earn interest from tax liens or profits from selling properties, you can use these funds to purchase additional liens or deeds. This can allow you to increase the size of your portfolio without requiring additional capital.

Another approach is to leverage your equity from other properties, as discussed in the previous chapter. By borrowing against the equity in your properties, you can access additional capital to invest in more tax liens or deeds.

It's also important to consider the timing of your scaling efforts. Tax lien and deed investing is cyclical, with certain times of the year offering more opportunities than others. By understanding these cycles, you can time your investments to take advantage of peak periods.

In addition to increasing the size of your portfolio, scaling can also involve moving into new markets or types of investments. For example, you might start by investing in tax liens and then move into tax deeds as you gain experience. Or you might start in your local market and then expand into other states or regions.

Scaling your investment portfolio is a key strategy for achieving long-term success in tax lien and deed investing. By reinvesting your returns, leveraging your equity, and timing your investments, you can increase the size of your portfolio and enhance your potential returns. However, it's important to approach scaling in a strategic and measured way, considering the potential risks as well as the potential rewards. As always, it's advisable to consult with a financial advisor or investment professional to ensure you're making sound investment decisions.

2. Diversifying Investments

Diversification is a critical strategy for long-term success in tax lien and deed investing. By spreading your investments across a variety of liens or deeds, you can reduce risk and increase your potential for steady, reliable returns.

Diversification in tax lien and deed investing can take several forms. One is diversification by location. Investing in tax liens or deeds in different geographic areas can protect you from local economic downturns or real estate market fluctuations. If property values decline in one area, your investments in other areas may still perform well.

Another form of diversification is investing in different types of properties. Residential properties, commercial properties, and vacant land all offer different risk and return profiles. By investing in a mix of property types, you can balance these risks and returns.

Diversification can also involve investing in both tax liens and tax deeds. While these investments are similar, they also have important differences. Tax liens offer the potential for steady interest income, while tax deeds offer the potential for larger, lump-sum returns. By investing in both, you can balance these different types of returns.

However, diversification is not just about spreading risk. It's also about maximizing opportunities. Different locations, property types, and investment types offer different opportunities for profit.

By diversifying, you can take advantage of a wider range of these opportunities.

While diversification can reduce risk and enhance returns, it also requires careful management. Investing in a variety of liens or deeds means keeping track of more investments, each with its own details and requirements. It's important to have systems in place to manage this complexity, such as a reliable method for tracking your investments and a clear strategy for managing your portfolio.

It's also important to remember that diversification is not a guarantee against loss. Even a diversified portfolio can lose value if property values decline broadly or if there are changes in tax laws or other factors. Therefore, it's important to regularly review and adjust your portfolio as needed.

Diversification is a key strategy for long-term success in tax lien and deed investing. By investing in a variety of locations, property types, and investment types, you can reduce risk and increase your potential for steady, reliable returns. However, diversification requires careful management and ongoing review to ensure your portfolio remains balanced and aligned with your investment goals. As always, it's advisable to consult with a financial advisor or investment professional to ensure you're making sound investment decisions.

3. Investing in Multiple Markets

Investing in multiple markets is another strategy that can contribute to long-term success in tax lien and deed investing. This approach involves spreading your investments across different geographic areas or jurisdictions. By diversifying your investments in this way, you can reduce the risk associated with any single market and potentially access a wider range of investment opportunities.

Each market has its own unique characteristics, including property values, tax laws, and economic conditions. These factors can significantly impact the performance of tax lien and deed investments. By investing in multiple markets, you can spread your risk across these different environments. If one market performs poorly, your investments in other markets may still provide solid returns.

Investing in multiple markets can also provide opportunities for higher returns. Some markets may offer higher interest rates on tax liens or lower property prices for tax deeds. By exploring different markets, you can identify and take advantage of these potentially lucrative opportunities.

However, investing in multiple markets also presents challenges. Each market has its own rules and procedures for tax lien and deed investing. You'll need to understand and navigate these rules in each market where you invest. This can require significant research and due diligence.

In addition, managing investments in multiple markets can be complex. You'll need to track and manage multiple sets of investments, each with its own timelines, requirements, and potential issues. This can require a high level of organization and attention to detail.

Despite these challenges, the potential benefits of investing in multiple markets can make it a worthwhile strategy. To successfully invest in multiple markets, it's important to conduct thorough research and due diligence. Understand the rules and characteristics of each market, and be prepared to manage the complexity of multiple sets of investments.

Technology can be a valuable tool in this regard. There are many software programs and online platforms that can help you research different markets, track your investments, and manage your portfolio. These tools can make it easier to invest in multiple markets and manage the associated complexity.

Investing in multiple markets can be a powerful strategy for long-term success in tax lien and deed investing. It can provide both risk reduction and potential for higher returns. However, it requires thorough research, careful management, and potentially the use of technology tools. As always, it's advisable to consult with a financial advisor or investment professional to ensure you're making sound investment decisions.

4. Building a Passive Income Stream

Building a passive income stream is one of the most appealing aspects of tax lien and deed investing. Passive income is money you earn with little to no daily effort, and it can provide financial stability and freedom. With tax lien and deed investing, you can build a passive income stream through the interest payments from tax liens or the rental income from properties acquired through tax deeds.

Tax liens are particularly well-suited for generating passive income. When you invest in a tax lien, you're essentially lending money to a property owner who has failed to pay their property taxes. In return, you receive the right to collect interest on the amount owed. This interest can provide a steady stream of income with little ongoing effort on your part.

The rate of interest you earn on a tax lien can be quite high compared to other types of investments, often ranging from 8% to 36% per year depending on the jurisdiction. This high rate of return can make tax lien investing a lucrative strategy for building a passive income stream.

In addition to the interest income from tax liens, you can also generate passive income from properties acquired through tax deeds. If you acquire a property through a tax deed and choose to rent it out, the rental income can provide a steady cash flow. This can be an effective way to generate passive income, particularly if property values and rental rates are high in the area where you invest.

However, building a passive income stream through tax lien and deed investing requires careful planning and strategy. It's important to invest in liens or deeds that offer a good potential return and to manage your investments effectively. This can involve researching properties and markets, bidding wisely at auctions, and managing properties or liens effectively.

It's also important to be aware of the potential risks and challenges. For example, the property owner may fail to pay off the lien, in which case you may need to foreclose on the property to recover your investment. In the case of tax deeds, you may need to manage the property or deal with tenants, which can require time and effort.

Building a passive income stream is a key strategy for long-term success in tax lien and deed investing. By investing wisely and managing your investments effectively, you can generate a steady stream of income with little ongoing effort. However, it's important to be aware of the potential risks and challenges, and to approach this strategy with care and diligence. As always, it's advisable to consult with a financial advisor or investment professional to ensure you're making sound investment decisions.

5. Managing Your Portfolio Like a Pro

Managing your portfolio like a pro is a key component of long-term success in tax lien and deed investing. This involves not just selecting and purchasing investments, but also monitoring them, making strategic decisions, and adjusting your portfolio as needed.

One of the first steps in managing your portfolio is tracking your investments. This involves keeping detailed records of each investment, including the purchase price, the interest rate or potential return, and any payments or income received. It also involves monitoring the status of each investment, such as whether a tax lien has been paid off or a property acquired through a tax deed has been sold.

Another important aspect of portfolio management is analysis. This involves evaluating the performance of your investments and comparing them to your goals or benchmarks. For example, you might compare the return on your tax lien investments to the interest rate you could earn on a high-yield savings account or other investment. This analysis can help you identify underperforming investments and make informed decisions about buying or selling.

Strategic decision-making is another key part of portfolio management. This can involve deciding when to sell a property acquired through a tax deed, whether to bid on a particular tax lien, or how much to bid. These decisions should be based on careful analysis and a clear understanding of your investment goals.

Finally, managing your portfolio like a pro involves adjusting your portfolio as needed. This can involve selling off underperforming investments, investing in new opportunities, or rebalancing your portfolio to maintain the right mix of investments. It's important to review your portfolio regularly and make adjustments as needed to stay aligned with your investment goals.

Managing your portfolio like a pro is a key strategy for long-term success in tax lien and deed investing. By tracking your investments, analyzing their performance, making strategic decisions, and adjusting your portfolio as needed, you can optimize your returns and achieve your investment goals. As always, it's advisable to consult with a financial advisor or investment professional to ensure you're making sound investment decisions.

Chapter 11

ADVANCED TECHNIQUES FOR EXPERIENCED INVESTORS

1. How to Buy Properties Before They Go to Auction

Buying properties before they go to auction is an advanced technique that can provide experienced investors with unique opportunities. This approach involves identifying properties that are likely to be sold at a tax deed auction and negotiating a purchase directly with the property owner. If successful, you can acquire the property without having to compete with other bidders at an auction.

The key to this strategy is research. You need to identify properties that are delinquent on their property taxes and are nearing the point of being sold at a tax deed auction. This information is typically available from the local tax collector or county clerk, either online or in person. Once you've identified potential properties, you can research the property and the owner to assess the potential value and likelihood of a successful purchase.

Once you've identified a potential property, the next step is to contact the property owner. This can be a delicate process, as the owner is likely under financial stress. It's important to approach the owner with empathy and respect, offering a solution that can help them avoid losing their property at auction. If the owner is interested, you can negotiate a purchase price that is agreeable to both parties.

There are several advantages to buying properties before they go to auction. First, you can potentially acquire the property at a lower price than you would at an auction, where competition can drive up prices. Second, you can avoid the uncertainty and risk of bidding at an auction. Third, you can potentially acquire the property more quickly, as you don't have to wait for the auction date.

However, this strategy also comes with challenges. It requires significant research and due diligence to identify potential properties and assess their value. It also requires negotiation skills and the ability to navigate potentially sensitive conversations with property owners. Finally, there is always the risk that the owner will refuse to sell or that you will be unable to agree on a purchase price.

Buying properties before they go to auction is an advanced technique that can offer experienced investors unique opportunities. By conducting thorough research and approaching property owners with empathy and respect, you can potentially acquire properties at a lower cost and with less competition than at an auction. However, this strategy requires significant effort and skill, and it comes with its own risks and challenges. As always, it's advisable to consult with a real estate professional or attorney to ensure you're making sound investment decisions.

2. Insider Secrets to Doubling Returns

Doubling returns in tax lien and deed investing is a goal that many experienced investors strive for. While there are no guaranteed methods to achieve this, there are several insider secrets that can significantly enhance your potential returns.

One strategy is to target high-interest tax liens. In some jurisdictions, the interest rate on tax liens can be as high as 18% to 36% per year. By focusing on these high-interest liens, you can potentially double your investment in a few years, assuming the property owner pays off the lien.

Another strategy is to invest in tax deeds for properties that are undervalued or have high potential for appreciation. If you can acquire a property at a tax deed auction for significantly less than its market value, and if the property value increases over time, you can potentially double your investment when you sell the property.

A third strategy is to leverage your investments. This involves using borrowed money to invest in more tax liens or deeds than you could with your own capital alone. By leveraging your investments, you can potentially earn returns on a larger amount of capital, which can amplify your overall returns.

A fourth strategy is to reinvest your returns. As you earn interest from tax liens or profits from selling properties, you can use these funds to invest in more tax liens or deeds. This can create a compounding effect, where your returns generate additional returns, potentially doubling your investment over time.

However, it's important to note that these strategies come with increased risk. High-interest tax liens often involve properties with lower values or higher risks, and investing in undervalued properties requires a keen understanding of the real estate market. Leveraging your investments can amplify your potential losses as well as your potential gains, and reinvesting your returns means tying up your capital in your investments.

There are several strategies that experienced investors can use to potentially double their returns in tax lien and deed investing. These include targeting high-interest tax liens, investing in undervalued properties, leveraging your investments, and reinvesting your returns. However, these strategies come with increased risk and require a high level of skill and knowledge. As always, it's advisable to consult with a financial advisor or investment professional to ensure you're making sound investment decisions.

3. Using Technology to Enhance Your Investments (the most up-to-date and recent information possible)

In today's digital age, technology can play a significant role in enhancing your tax lien and deed investments. From research and due diligence to bidding and portfolio management, there are numerous ways that technology can streamline processes, provide valuable insights, and ultimately increase your returns.

One of the most important ways technology can enhance your investments is through online research tools. Many counties now offer online databases of tax liens and deeds, making it easier than ever to research potential investments. These databases can provide detailed information on properties, including their assessed value, tax history, and any outstanding liens or encumbrances. This information can be crucial in assessing the potential value and risk of an investment.

In addition to county databases, there are also numerous online platforms and software programs designed specifically for tax lien and deed investors. These tools can provide advanced features such as property analysis, market trends, and investment tracking. Some platforms even offer predictive analytics, using algorithms and machine learning to forecast property values and investment returns.

Another way technology can enhance your investments is through online auctions. Many counties now conduct their tax lien and deed auctions online, allowing investors to bid from anywhere in the world. This can provide access to a wider range of investment opportunities and can also make the bidding process more efficient.

Technology can also aid in portfolio management. There are numerous software programs and apps available that can help you track your investments, monitor their performance, and manage your portfolio. These tools can provide real-time updates, generate reports, and even send alerts for important dates or events, such as the redemption period for a tax lien.

Finally, technology can also facilitate communication and networking. Online forums, social media groups, and virtual events can provide opportunities to connect with other investors, share insights, and learn from others' experiences. These connections can be invaluable in staying informed about market trends, learning new strategies, and navigating the challenges of tax lien and deed investing.

Technology can significantly enhance your tax lien and deed investments. By leveraging online research tools, participating in online auctions, using portfolio management software, and connecting with other investors online, you can streamline your processes, make more informed decisions, and ultimately increase your returns. However, it's important to remember that technology is a tool, not a substitute for thorough research, due diligence, and sound investment decisions. As always, it's advisable to consult with a financial advisor or investment professional to ensure you're making sound investment decisions.

4. Building Relationships with Local Authorities

Building relationships with local authorities is an often-overlooked but crucial aspect of successful tax lien and deed investing. These relationships can provide valuable insights, facilitate smoother transactions, and even open up unique investment opportunities.

Local authorities, such as county tax collectors, county clerks, and local government officials, play a key role in tax lien and deed investing. They are responsible for administering property taxes, managing tax delinquencies, and conducting tax lien and deed auctions. As such, they can provide valuable information and assistance to investors.

Building relationships with local authorities begins with respect and professionalism. It's important to approach these individuals with courtesy, understanding that they are often busy and under pressure. Be prepared, know what questions to ask, and respect their time. This will help establish a positive rapport and open lines of communication.

Regular contact is also important in building these relationships. Attend local government meetings, participate in tax lien and deed auctions, and make a point of introducing yourself and engaging in conversation. Over time, this regular contact can help you become a familiar and trusted figure.

These relationships can provide several benefits. Local authorities can provide insider knowledge about the local real estate market, upcoming auctions, and specific properties. They can also provide advice and guidance on local rules and procedures, helping you navigate the complexities of tax lien and deed investing.

In some cases, building relationships with local authorities can also lead to unique investment opportunities. For example, some counties offer "over the counter" tax liens or deeds, which are liens or deeds that were not sold at auction and can be purchased directly from the county. Local authorities may also be aware of upcoming changes in local laws or policies that could impact your investments.

However, it's important to approach these relationships with integrity and ethical conduct. Avoid any actions that could be perceived as attempting to gain unfair advantage or influence. Always conduct your business in a transparent and ethical manner.

Building relationships with local authorities is a valuable strategy for experienced tax lien and deed investors. These relationships can provide valuable insights, facilitate smoother transactions, and open up unique investment opportunities. However, it's important to approach these relationships with respect, professionalism, and integrity. As always, it's advisable to consult with a financial advisor or investment professional to ensure you're making sound investment decisions.

5. Staying Ahead of the Competition

In the world of tax lien and deed investing, competition can be fierce. Investors are always on the lookout for profitable opportunities, and at times, it can feel like a race to secure the best deals. Staying ahead of the competition requires a combination of knowledge, strategy, and adaptability.

Knowledge is your first line of defense against competition. The more you know about the market, the laws, the process, and the properties, the better positioned you are to make sound investment decisions. This knowledge can give you an edge in identifying and securing profitable opportunities before others even know they exist. Continuous learning and staying updated with market trends and changes in laws and regulations is crucial.

Your strategy is another key factor in staying ahead. This includes your approach to research, bidding, managing your portfolio, and more. A well-planned and executed strategy can help you secure deals more efficiently and effectively than competitors who may be less organized or strategic.

Adaptability is equally important. The world of tax lien and deed investing is dynamic, with market conditions, laws, and opportunities constantly changing. Being able to adapt your strategy in response to these changes can keep you one step ahead of the competition. This might mean exploring new markets, adjusting your bidding strategy, or diversifying your portfolio.

Networking can also give you a competitive edge. Building relationships with local authorities, real estate professionals, and other investors can provide valuable insights and opportunities. These relationships can give you access to information and deals that may not be readily available to others.

Lastly, leveraging technology can greatly enhance your competitive edge. From research tools and online auctions to portfolio management software, technology can streamline your processes, provide valuable insights, and save you time and effort. In a competitive market, these efficiencies can make the difference between securing a deal or missing out.

Staying ahead of the competition in tax lien and deed investing requires knowledge, strategy, adaptability, networking, and the effective use of technology. By developing these areas, you can position yourself for success and secure profitable deals in this competitive market. As always, it's advisable to consult with a financial advisor or investment professional to ensure you're making sound investment decisions.

Chapter 12

REAL-LIFE SUCCESS STORIES AND CASE STUDIES

1. Inspiring Success Stories

The world of tax lien and deed investing is filled with inspiring success stories that serve as powerful examples of what can be achieved with knowledge, strategy, and perseverance. These stories provide valuable insights into the potential rewards of this type of investing, and they can serve as a source of motivation and inspiration for both new and experienced investors.

One such story involves a woman named Lisa, a single mother who was looking for a way to build wealth and provide for her family. With limited capital but a strong desire to improve her financial situation, Lisa turned to tax lien investing. She started small, investing in a few liens in her local area. Over time, she was able to grow her portfolio and generate a steady stream of passive income. Today, Lisa is financially independent and able to provide a comfortable life for her family, all thanks to her investments in tax liens.

Another inspiring story involves a man named Tom, a retired engineer who was looking for a way to supplement his retirement income. Tom discovered tax deed investing and was drawn to the potential for high returns. He invested in a tax deed for a property that was significantly undervalued, and after a few years, he was able to sell the property for a substantial profit. Tom's story demonstrates the potential for significant returns in tax deed investing, even for those who are new to the field.

There's also the story of a young couple, Sarah and John, who were looking for a way to build wealth and secure their financial future. They decided to invest in tax liens and deeds as a way to diversify their investment portfolio. Despite some initial challenges, they were able to learn from their experiences and refine their strategy. Today, they have a diverse portfolio of tax liens and deeds that provides them with a steady income and a solid financial foundation.

These stories are just a few examples of the many individuals who have achieved success through tax lien and deed investing. They demonstrate that with the right knowledge, strategy, and perseverance, it's possible to build wealth and achieve financial independence through this type of investing. These stories serve as a powerful reminder of the potential rewards of tax lien and deed investing, and they provide inspiration for those who are considering this path.

2. Overcoming Challenges

In the journey of tax lien and deed investing, overcoming challenges is often a significant part of the story. These challenges can take many forms, from navigating complex regulations to dealing with unexpected issues with properties. However, it's through facing and overcoming these challenges that investors often gain the most valuable insights and experiences.

Consider the story of Mark, a seasoned real estate investor who decided to venture into tax lien investing. Mark was initially drawn to the high potential returns and the passive nature of tax lien investing. However, he quickly found that the process was more complex than he had anticipated. He faced challenges in understanding the different laws and regulations in various counties, and he made some costly mistakes in his early investments. However, Mark didn't let these challenges deter him. Instead, he took them as learning opportunities. He sought advice from more experienced investors, attended workshops, and spent countless hours studying the laws and regulations. Over time, Mark was able to overcome these challenges and become a successful tax lien investor.

Another example is the story of Linda, a retiree who turned to tax deed investing as a way to supplement her retirement income. Linda purchased a tax deed for a property that she thought was a great deal. However, she later discovered that the property had significant structural issues that required costly repairs. This was a major setback, but Linda was determined to overcome this challenge. She worked with a contractor to fix the issues and even learned some basic home repair skills herself. After many months of hard work, Linda was able to sell the property at a profit.

Then there's the story of Alex and Maria, a young couple who started investing in tax liens and deeds as a way to build wealth. They faced numerous challenges along the way, from bidding wars at auctions to dealing with uncooperative property owners. However, they remained persistent and adaptable, learning from each challenge and continuously refining their strategy. Today, Alex and Maria have a successful portfolio of tax liens and deeds, and they credit their success to their ability to overcome challenges.

These stories highlight the challenges that can arise in tax lien and deed investing and the resilience required to overcome them. They show that while this type of investing can be complex and challenging, it's also possible to turn these challenges into opportunities for learning and growth. These stories serve as a reminder that with perseverance, adaptability, and a willingness to learn, it's possible to overcome challenges and achieve success in tax lien and deed investing. As always, it's advisable to consult with a financial advisor or investment professional to ensure you're making sound investment decisions.

3. Turning Small Investments into Large Profits

One of the most appealing aspects of tax lien and deed investing is the potential to turn small investments into large profits. This is particularly attractive to investors who may not have large amounts of capital to invest but are eager to build wealth and achieve financial independence. Numerous success stories illustrate this potential, providing both inspiration and valuable lessons for investors.

Take, for example, the story of Sam, a recent college graduate with limited capital. Sam was interested in investing but felt discouraged by the high entry costs of traditional real estate investing. However, when he learned about tax lien investing, he saw an opportunity. He started small, investing in a few tax liens in his local county. Over time, as the liens were paid off with interest, Sam reinvested the returns into more liens. This compounding effect, combined with Sam's diligent research and careful selection of liens, allowed him to grow his initial small investment into a substantial portfolio.

Then there's the story of Rachel, a single mother who was looking for ways to secure her financial future. Rachel started investing in tax deeds with a small amount of savings. Her first purchase was a small, run-down property that she bought at a tax deed auction for a fraction of its market value. Rachel put in the work to renovate the property herself, then rented it out for a steady income. Over time, the property's value increased significantly, turning Rachel's small investment into a large profit.

Another compelling story is that of Mike, a middle-aged office worker who was looking for ways to supplement his income. Mike started investing in tax liens with a small amount of his savings. He focused on liens with high interest rates and was diligent in his research to ensure he was making sound investments. Over time, as the liens were paid off with interest, Mike's small investment grew into a substantial sum.

These stories illustrate the potential of tax lien and deed investing to turn small investments into large profits. They show that with careful research, strategic investing, and a bit of patience, it's possible to achieve significant returns, even with a small initial investment.

However, it's important to note that these success stories are not the norm for all investors. Tax lien and deed investing involves risk, and there's no guarantee of returns. It requires diligent research, careful decision-making, and an understanding of the local real estate market and tax laws. Furthermore, it's crucial to only invest money that you can afford to lose, as there's always the possibility that a lien won't be paid off or a property won't sell for a profit.

While tax lien and deed investing has the potential to turn small investments into large profits, it's not a guaranteed path to wealth. Success in this field requires knowledge, strategy, patience, and a willingness to take on risk. As always, it's advisable to consult with a financial advisor or investment professional to ensure you're making sound investment decisions.

4. Strategies That Worked

In the world of tax lien and deed investing, there are countless strategies that investors can employ. However, the most successful investors often have specific strategies that they've honed over time, which have proven to be effective in generating profits. These strategies can provide valuable insights for both new and experienced investors.

Consider the story of Jennifer, a seasoned real estate investor who decided to expand her portfolio by investing in tax liens. Jennifer's strategy involved targeting liens on properties in desirable locations. She reasoned that these properties were more likely to be redeemed, earning her the interest on the lien. Additionally, if the lien wasn't redeemed, she would acquire a property in a prime location. This strategy proved to be successful, yielding consistent returns and even a few valuable properties.

Another example is the strategy employed by David, a retiree who turned to tax deed investing as a way to supplement his retirement income. David's strategy involved purchasing tax deeds for properties that were undervalued or in need of minor repairs. He would then invest in necessary renovations and sell the properties at a profit. Despite the additional work and investment required, this strategy allowed David to significantly increase his returns.

Then there's the strategy of Emma, a young professional who started investing in tax liens as a side hustle. Emma's strategy was to focus on liens with high interest rates. She would thoroughly research each property and its owner to assess the likelihood of the lien being redeemed. This strategy required a significant amount of time and effort, but it paid off in the form of high returns.

Finally, consider the strategy of Mike and Lisa, a couple who decided to invest in tax deeds as a way to diversify their investment portfolio. Their strategy involved purchasing tax deeds for properties in areas with strong rental markets. They would then rent out the properties, providing them with a steady stream of passive income. Over time, as property values increased, they also saw significant appreciation in their portfolio.

These stories illustrate a range of strategies that have proven successful in tax lien and deed investing. They highlight the importance of having a clear strategy based on careful research, thorough analysis, and a solid understanding of the market and the laws. They also underscore the fact that there's no one-size-fits-all strategy in this field. What works for one investor might not work for another, and success often involves adapting and refining your strategy over time.

Successful tax lien and deed investing requires a well-thought-out and executed strategy. Whether it's targeting liens with high interest rates, investing in undervalued properties, or focusing on properties in strong rental markets, the key is to find a strategy that aligns with your goals, resources, and risk tolerance. As always, it's advisable to consult with a financial advisor or investment professional to ensure you're making sound investment decisions.

5. What You Can Learn from Their Journeys

The journeys of successful tax lien and deed investors offer invaluable lessons for those who aspire to follow in their footsteps. These lessons, gleaned from real-life experiences, can provide guidance, inspiration, and practical insights for both new and experienced investors.

One of the most important lessons is the value of knowledge and education. Almost every successful investor's journey underscores the importance of understanding the ins and outs of tax lien and deed investing, from the legal aspects to the nuances of different markets. This knowledge forms the foundation of successful investing, enabling investors to make informed decisions, mitigate risks, and maximize returns.

Another key lesson is the importance of due diligence. The stories of successful investors often highlight how thorough research and careful analysis can lead to profitable investments. Whether it's assessing the value of a property, understanding the local real estate market, or evaluating the likelihood of a lien being redeemed, due diligence is a critical part of the process.

The journeys of successful investors also underscore the value of patience and perseverance. Tax lien and deed investing is not a get-rich-quick scheme. It requires time, effort, and sometimes, dealing with setbacks and challenges. However, those who persevere often reap the rewards in the form of steady returns and profitable investments.

Furthermore, these journeys highlight the importance of having a clear strategy. Whether it's focusing on high-interest liens, investing in undervalued properties, or targeting properties in strong rental markets, having a well-defined strategy can guide your investment decisions and increase your chances of success.

Finally, these stories often illustrate the power of adaptability. The world of tax lien and deed investing is dynamic, with market conditions, laws, and opportunities constantly changing. Successful investors are those who can adapt their strategies in response to these changes, seizing new opportunities and navigating challenges as they arise.

The journeys of successful tax lien and deed investors offer valuable lessons for those who aspire to succeed in this field. From the importance of knowledge and due diligence to the value of patience, perseverance, a clear strategy, and adaptability, these lessons can guide and inspire investors on their own journeys. As always, it's advisable to consult with a financial advisor or investment professional to ensure you're making sound investment decisions.

CONCLUSION

As we draw this book to a close, it's time to reflect on the journey we've taken together. We've explored the ins and outs of tax lien and deed investing, delved into the complexities of laws and regulations, and examined the strategies that can lead to success. We've also looked at the potential pitfalls and how to avoid them, and we've heard inspiring stories from those who have achieved success in this field.

This journey has been filled with valuable insights and practical advice. However, the most important step is yet to come: taking action. Knowledge is a powerful tool, but it's only through action that you can truly reap the benefits of tax lien and deed investing. Whether you're a new investor looking to dip your toes into the world of real estate investing, an experienced investor seeking to diversify your portfolio, or a retiree in search of a steady income stream, the time to act is now.

Start by setting clear goals for your investing journey. What do you hope to achieve through tax lien and deed investing? Are you seeking a passive income stream, looking to acquire properties at a discount, or aiming to achieve high returns? Your goals will guide your strategy and help you make informed investment decisions.

Next, dedicate time to education and research. The more you understand about tax lien and deed investing, the better equipped you'll be to navigate this complex field. Attend workshops, read books, join online communities, and seek advice from experienced investors.

Then, start small. You don't need a large amount of capital to get started in tax lien and deed investing. Start with a few investments, learn from your experiences, and gradually grow your portfolio over time. Remember, patience and perseverance are key in this field.

Looking ahead, the future of tax lien and deed investing looks promising. As we move into 2024 and 2025, several trends are likely to shape the landscape of this field. Technology will continue to play a significant role, with online auctions, digital research tools, and portfolio management software making it easier and more efficient for investors to manage their investments.

Furthermore, as more people seek alternative investments and passive income opportunities, demand for tax liens and deeds is likely to increase. This could lead to more competition, but also more opportunities for savvy investors.

Finally, changes in laws and regulations could also impact the field of tax lien and deed investing. It's crucial to stay updated on these changes and understand how they could affect your investments.

The journey to successful tax lien and deed investing is a journey of knowledge, action, and adaptability. It's a journey that requires patience and perseverance, but also offers the potential for significant rewards. As you embark on this journey, remember that the key to success lies in your hands. You have the power to shape your financial future, and with the knowledge and insights gained from this book, you're well-equipped to do so.

So, take that first step. Start your journey today. The world of tax lien and deed investing awaits, and I, Robert Newton, am excited to see where your journey will take you.

Made in the USA
Columbia, SC
06 January 2025